access to history

REACTION &
REVOLUTIONS:
RUSSIA 1881–1924

Second Edition

Michael Lynch

D0230023

Hodder & Stoughton

A MEMBER OF THE HODDER HEADLINE GROUP

Acknowledgements

The front cover shows V.I. Lenin at the Tribune by A Gerasimov, reproduced coutesy of Novosti (London).

The publishers would like to thank the following individuals, institutions and companies for permission to reproduce copyright illustrations in this book:

David King Collection page 8, Houghton Library page 70; Hulton Getty pages 88 and 120; Novosti (London) pages 39 and 68; Russian Pictorial Collection/Hoover Institution Archives page 94.

The publishers would also like to thank the following for permission to reproduce material in this book:

John Murray (Publishers) Ltd for the extract from *Nicholas II Emperor of All the Russians* by Dominic Lieven, 1993; RICHARD PIPES: *The Russian Revolution*. First published in 1990 in America by Alfred A Knopf and in Great Britain by The Harvill Press. Copyright © Richard Pipes, 1990. Reproduced by permission of The Harvill Press; Reproduced by permission of Penguin Books Ltd, *An Economic History of the USSR 1917–1991* by Alec Nove (Allen Lane, The Penguin Prees 1969, Third Edition, 1992) © Alec Nove, 1969, 1972, 1976, 1982, 1982, 1989, 1992 and *The Eastern Front 1914–1917* by Noman Stone (Penguin Books, 1998) Copyright © Norman Stone, 1988; Random House Group Ltd for the extracts from *A People's Tragedy The Russian Revolution 1891-1924* by Orlando Figes, Jonathan Cape, 1996.

Every effort has been made to trace and acknowledge ownership of copyright. The publishers will be glad to make suitable arrangements with any copyright holders whom it has not been possible to contact.

Orders: please contact Bookpoint Ltd, 130 Milton Park, Abingdon, Oxon OX14 4SB. Telephone: (44) 01235 827720, Fax: (44) 01235 400454. Lines are open from 9.00–6.00, Monday to Saturday, with a 24 hour message answering service. You can also order through our website: www.hodderheadline.co.uk

British Library Cataloguing in Publication Data
A catalogue record for this title is available from The British Library

ISBN 0 340 75384 6

First published 1992
Impression number   10 9 8 7 6
Year   2005 2004

Copyright © 1992, 2000 Michael Lynch

Typeset by Fakenham Photosetting Limited, Fakenham, Norfolk.
Printed in Great Britain for Hodder & Stoughton Educational, a division of Hodder Headline, 338 Euston Road, London NW1 3BH by CPI Bath.

Contents

Preface

To the general reader

Although the *Access to History* series has been designed with the needs of students studying the subject at higher examination levels very much in mind, it also has a great deal to offer the general reader. The main body of the text (i.e. ignoring the 'Study Guides' at the ends of chapters) forms a readable and yet stimulating survey of a coherent topic as studied by historians. However, each author's aim has not merely been to provide a clear explanation of what happened in the past (to interest and inform): it has also been assumed that most readers wish to be stimulated into thinking further about the topic and to form opinions of their own about the significance of the events that are described and discussed (to be challenged). Thus, although no prior knowledge of the topic is expected on the reader's part, she or he is treated as an intelligent and thinking person throughout. The author tends to share ideas and possibilities with the reader, rather than passing on numbers of so-called 'historical truths'.

To the student reader

Although advantage has been taken of the publication of a second edition to ensure the results of recent research are reflected in the text, the main alteration from the first edition is the inclusion of new features, and the modification of existing ones, aimed at assisting you in your study of the topic at AS level, A level and Higher. Two features are designed to assist you during your first reading of a chapter. The *Points to Consider* section following each chapter title is intended to focus your attention on the main theme(s) of the chapter, and the issues box following most section headings alerts you to the question or questions to be dealt with in the section. The *Working on . . .* section at the end of each chapter suggests ways of gaining maximum benefit from the chapter.

There are many ways in which the series can be used by students studying History at a higher level. It will, therefore, be worthwhile thinking about your own study strategy before you start your work on this book. Obviously, your strategy will vary depending on the aim you have in mind, and the time for study that is available to you.

If, for example, you want to acquire a general overview of the topic in the shortest possible time, the following approach will probably be the most effective:

1. Read chapter 1. As you do so, keep in mind the issues raised in the *Points to Consider* section.

2. Read the *Points to Consider* section at the beginning of chapter 2 and decide whether it is necessary for you to read this chapter.
3. If it is, read the chapter, stopping at each heading or sub-heading to note down the main points that have been made. Often, the best way of doing this is to answer the question(s) posed in the Issues boxes.
4. Repeat stage 2 (and stage 3 where appropriate) for all the other chapters.

If, however, your aim is to gain a thorough grasp of the topic, taking however much time is necessary to do so, you may benefit from carrying out the same procedure with each chapter, as follows:

1. Try to read the chapter in one sitting. As you do this, bear in mind any advice given in the *Points to Consider* section.
2. Study the flow diagram at the end of the chapter, ensuring that you understand the general 'shape' of what you have just read.
3. Read the *Working on ...* section and decide what further work you need to do on the chapter. In particularly important sections of the book, this is likely to involve reading the chapter a second time and stopping at each heading and sub-heading to think about (and probably to write a summary of) what you have just read.
4. Attempt the *Source-based questions* section. It will sometimes be sufficient to think through your answers, but additional understanding will often be gained by forcing yourself to write them down.

When you have finished the main chapters of the book, study the 'Further Reading' section and decide what additional reading (if any) you will do on the topic.

This book has been designed to help make your studies both enjoyable and successful. If you can think of ways in which this could have been done more effectively, please contact us. In the meantime, we hope that you will gain greatly from your study of History.

Keith Randell & Robert Pearce

1 Introduction

POINTS TO CONSIDER

In 1881 Russia was an empire, ruled over by an all-powerful tsar. By 1924 it had become a Union of Soviet Socialist Republics, ruled over by an all-powerful political party. Such a remarkable transformation involved profound political, social and economic changes. This book describes these changes and analyses why they occurred, paying particular attention to the events of 1917 – the year of the Bolshevik Revolution. In this opening chapter the key features of the period are briefly described. A cross-reference is given in brackets to the chapters where the themes are explored in detail. The chapter then provides an introduction to the rest of the book by describing the main features of imperial Russia. The concluding section looks at the question of why it was so difficult to achieve genuine reform in Russia.

1 Outline of the Period, 1881–1924

1881–95 – the years of reaction and growing resistance

In reaction to the assassination of the reforming tsar, Alexander II, by a group of revolutionaries, the government followed a policy of severe repression. Its aim was the traditional one of crushing all political opposition (Chapter 2). In spite of the regime's severity, a number of reforming and revolutionary parties had come into being by the end of the century. These represented a range of opinions, from the wish to see the tsarist system reformed to the desire to see it swept away altogether (Chapter 3).

1893–1903 – 'the great spurt'

What had helped to stimulate reformers and revolutionaries alike was a rapid period of industrial growth in the 1890s, associated with the work of Sergei Witte, the minister of finance. This 'great spurt' seemed to offer a possibility that Russia might be able to throw off its economic backwardness (Chapter 2).

1904–14 – revolution and repression

Following Russia's disastrous showing in a war against Japan 1904–05, there occurred a series of nationwide disturbances, which were serious enough to be referred to as the 1905 Revolution. This obliged the government to make some concessions. A duma (parliament) was introduced and became a feature of the political scene until 1917.

However, the tsar, Nicholas II, had no intention of allowing the duma to become a genuine limitation on his autocratic powers. Between 1907 and 1914 its authority was increasingly eroded under the repressive policies of Peter Stolypin (Chapter 2).

1914–17 Imperial Russia at war

In 1914 Russia became involved in war with Germany and Austria–Hungary. This put a great strain on the nation's military and economic systems and raised searching political questions about the ability of the tsar and his government to lead the nation in time of crisis (Chapter 4).

The 1917 Revolution

Faced by economic disruption, military reverses in the field and mounting opposition at home, Nicholas II abdicated in the 'February Revolution' of 1917. He was replaced by the Provisional Government, the remnant of the old duma (Chapter 4). But from the beginning the new government was beset by major problems. It had, in effect, to share its authority with the Petrograd Soviet, a self-appointed council of soldiers, workers and peasants. The continuing war, food shortages, and rampant inflation under-mined the Provisional Government's efforts to create stability. In October, the Bolsheviks, the Marxist revolutionary party led by Lenin, who had returned to Russia on the fall of the tsar, mounted a successful coup against it (Chapter 5).

The Bolshevik Consolidation of Power, 1917–24

During the years following their seizure of power in 1917, Lenin and the Bolsheviks had to defend their revolution against the forces of reaction (generally referred to as the Whites) and to fight off attempted invasions of Soviet Russia by the western capitalist powers. They were successful in this and by the time of Lenin's death in 1924 they had crushed all forms of political opposition within Russia. They appeared to have laid the basis for the development of the USSR as the world's first socialist state (Chapter 6 and 7).

The significance of Russian history, 1881–1924

The character of the events that took place in Russia in these years has made the period one of unending debate. Why did Russia undergo such changes? Were they inevitable? What role did individuals play in the process? Could Russia have modernised its backward economic and social structure without undergoing revolution? Did the seizure of power in 1917 by a revolutionary Bolshevik Party mark the dawn of a new freedom for the Russian people, or did it simply replace one form of authoritarianism with another? In terms of its significance for the rest of the world, there is an even more important question. Was the Russian Revolution a model for all peoples seeking freedom and justice, or was it a fraudulent tyranny which led necessarily to misery and oppression? Such questions have long continued to excite fierce controversy among historians and analysts. As you work through this book you will find that it is questions such as these, and the often conflicting answers offered to them, that provide the major KEY ISSUES that are sign-posted for you along the way.

2 Imperial Russia

> **KEY ISSUE** Why had imperial Russia not modernised its governmental, political and economic systems?

a) Its Geography and People

In 1881 imperial Russia covered over eight million square miles, an area equivalent to two and a half times the size of the USA. At its widest, from west to east, it stretched for 5,000 miles; at its longest, north to south, it measured 2,000 miles. It covered a large part of two continents. European Russia extended eastward from the borders of Poland to the Urals mountain range. Asiatic Russia extended eastward from the Urals to the Pacific Ocean. The greater part of the

The major nationalities of the Russian Empire according to the census of 1897 (in millions, defined according to mother tongue)			
Great Russian	55.6	Lithuanian	1.2
Ukrainian	22.4	Armenian	1.2
Polish	7.9	Romanian/Moldavian	1.1
White Russian	5.8	Estonian	1.0
Jewish (defined by faith)	5.0	Mordvinian	1.0
Kirgiz/Kaisats	4.0	Georgian	0.8
Tartar	3.4	Tadzhik	0.3
Finnish	3.1	Turkmenian	0.3
German	1.8	Greek	0.2
Latvian	1.4	Bulgarian	0.2
Bashkir	1.3	Uzbekh	0.1

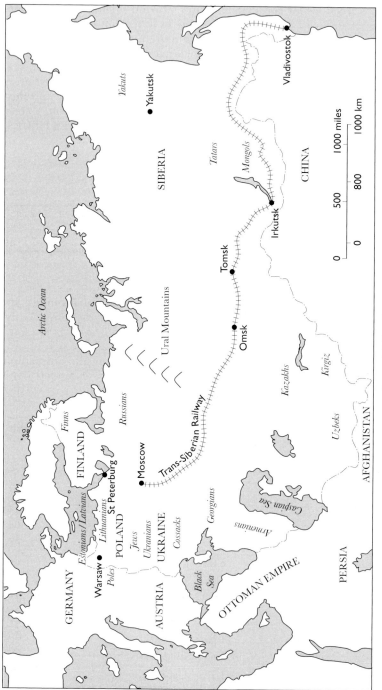

Imperial Russia.

population, which between 1815 and 1914 quadrupled from 40 million to 165 million, was concentrated in European Russia. It was in that part of the empire that the major historical developments had occurred and it was there that Russia's principal cities, Moscow and St Petersburg, the capital, were situated.

The sheer size of the Russian Empire tended to give an impression of great strength. This was misleading. The population contained a wide variety of peoples of different race, language, religion and culture. The difficulty of controlling such a variety of peoples over such a vast territory had long been a major problem for Russian governments.

b) The Tsarist Government

In theory, the peoples of the Russian Empire were governed by one person, the tsar (emperor). Since 1613 the Russian tsars had been members of the Romanov dynasty. By law and tradition, the tsar was the absolute ruler. Article I of the 'Fundamental Laws of the Empire', issued by Nicholas I in 1832, declared: 'The Emperor of all the Russias is an autocratic and unlimited monarch. God himself ordains that all must bow to his supreme power, not only out of fear but also out of conscience.'

There were three official bodies through which the tsar exercised his authority:

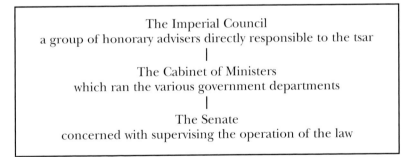

The Imperial Council
a group of honorary advisers directly responsible to the tsar
|
The Cabinet of Ministers
which ran the various government departments
|
The Senate
concerned with supervising the operation of the law

These bodies were much less powerful than their titles suggested. They were appointed, not elected, and their role was wholly advisory or administrative. In no way did they restrict the power of the tsar, whose word was the final authority in all matters of state and of law. That the tsar still claimed absolute authority was an indication of how little Russia had advanced politically. By the beginning of the twentieth century all the major western-European countries had some form of democratic or representative government. Not so Russia; although it had been frequently involved in European diplomatic and military affairs, it had remained outside the mainstream of European political thought. Progressive tsars such as Peter I (1683–1725), Catherine II (1762–96) and Alexander II (1855–81) had taken steps to modernise the country, but their reforms had not included the extension of political rights. In Russia in 1881 it was still a criminal offence to oppose the tsar or his government. There was no parliament, and political parties were not officially tolerated. State censorship was imposed on the press and on published books.

This did not prevent liberal ideas from seeping into Russia, but it did mean that they could not be openly expressed. The result was that supporters of reform or change had to go underground. In the nineteenth century there had grown up in Russia a wide variety of secret societies dedicated to political reform or revolution. These groups were frequently infiltrated by agents of the *Okhrana*, the tsar's secret police. As a result, raids, arrests, imprisonment and general harassment were regular occurrences.

Among Russia's governing classes there was a deeply ingrained prejudice against granting rights to the mass of the people. Over four-fifths of the population were peasants. They were predominantly illiterate and uneducated. Their sheer size as a social class and their uncivilised ways led to their being regarded with a mixture of fear and contempt by the governing elite, who believed that these dangerous 'dark masses' could be held in check only by severe repression. This was what Alexandra, the wife of the last tsar, Nicholas II (1894–1917), meant by saying that Russia needed always to be 'under the whip.' The denial of free speech tended to drive political activists towards extremism. The outstanding example of this was the assassination of Tsar Alexander II in 1881 by a terrorist group known as 'The People's Will' (see page 36). In a society in which state oppression vied with revolutionary terrorism, there was no moderate middle ground on which a tradition of ordered political debate could develop.

c) The Russian Orthodox Church

The tsars were fully supported in their claims to absolute authority by one of the great pillars of the Russian system, the Orthodox Church. This was a branch of Christianity which since the fifteenth century had been entirely independent of any outside authority, such as the papacy. Its detachment from foreign influence had given it an essentially Russian character. The beauty of its liturgy and music had long been an outstanding expression of Russian culture. However, by the late nineteenth century it had become an essentially conservative body, opposed to political change and wholly committed to the preservation of the tsarist system in its reactionary form. The Church did contain some priests who strongly sympathised with the political revolutionaries, but as an institution it used its spiritual authority to teach the Russian people that it was their duty to be totally obedient to the tsar as God's anointed. The catechism of the Church (the primer used for instructing the people in the essential points of the faith) included the statement that 'God commands us to love and obey from the inmost recesses of our heart every authority, and particularly the tsar'.

d) The Social and Economic Structure of Tsarist Russia
i) Social Classes
The striking features of the social structure were the comparatively small commercial, professional and working classes and the great preponderance of peasants in the population. This is illustrated in the accompanying pie-chart which shows the class distribution of the population, as measured by Russia's 1897 census.

Ruling class (tsar, court, and government)	0.5%
Upper class (nobility, higher clergy, military officers)	12.0%
Commercial class (merchants, factory owners, financiers)	1.5%
Working class (factory workers and small traders)	4.0%
Peasants (land dwellers and agricultural workers)	82.0%

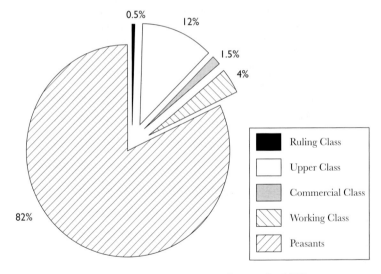

Class structure in tsarist Russia according to the 1897 census.

ii) Industry
The remarkable difference in size between the urban professional and working classes and the rural peasants illustrated a critical aspect of imperial Russia – its slow economic development. The low numbers of urban workers indicated that Russia had not experienced the major industrial expansion that had occurred in the nineteenth

УПРАВЛЯЮТЪ
НАШИМИ ДЕНЬГАМИ

МОЛЯТСЯ
ЗА НАСЪ

ѢДЯТЪ
ЗА НАСЪ

СТРѢЛЯЮТЪ
ВЪ НАСЪ

МЫ РАБОТАЕМЪ НА НИХЪ, А ОНИ —

A mocking socialist cartoon of 1900 showing the social pyramid in imperial
Russia. The Russian caption for each layer reads (in ascending order):
'We work for them while they . . .'
'. . . shoot at us.'
'. . . eat on our behalf.'
'. . . pray on our behalf.'
'. . . dispose of our money.'

century in such countries as Germany, Britain and the USA. This is not to say that Russia was entirely without industry. The Urals region produced considerable amounts of iron, and the chief western cities, Moscow and St Petersburg, had extensive textile factories. Most villages had a smelting-works, and most peasant homes engaged in some form of cottage-industry, producing wooden, flaxen or woollen goods to supplement their income from farming. However, these activities were all relatively small-scale. The sheer size of Russia and its undeveloped transport system had restricted industrial growth. A further limitation had been the absence of an effective banking system. Russia did not have access to the readily-available capital for investment in industry that had stimulated developments in other countries. These factors had discouraged the rise of entrepreneurialism, the dynamic, expansionist attitude that characterised western commercial and industrial activity in this period.

iii) Agriculture and the Peasantry

Russia's unenterprising industrial system was matched by its inefficient pattern of agriculture. Even though four-fifths of the population were peasants, a thriving agrarian economy had failed to develop. Indeed, the land in Russia was a source of national weakness rather than strength. The empire's vast acres were not all good farming country. Much of Russia lay too far north to enjoy a climate or a soil suitable for crop-growing or cattle-rearing. Arable farming was restricted mainly to the Black Earth region, the area of European Russia stretching from the Ukraine to Kazakhstan. In addition, the size of the peasant population created its own problems. There was simply not enough productive land to go round. The peasants were entitled to buy land under the terms of the Emancipation Decree of 1861, which had abolished serfdom (the Russian equivalent of landed slavery), but they invariably found its price excessively high. This was caused both by a scarcity of suitable farmland and by the government's taxation of property sales, imposed in order to raise the revenue needed to compensate the landowners for the loss of their serfs. The only way the peasants could raise the money to buy land was by borrowing from a special fund provided by the government. Consequently, those peasants who did manage to purchase property found themselves burdened with large mortgage repayments which would take them and their families generations to repay.

The high cost of land meant that few peasant families could afford to increase their acreage. The small areas that were purchased were normally subdivided into narrow strips in an attempt to provide each household within the family with some property, no matter how little. The result was greater inefficiency. The strip system, involving the use of antiquated farming implements and techniques, had long ago been abandoned in the agriculturally advanced nations. Its continuation in Russia was a major reason why the nation could not meet its food needs.

The existence in the second half of the nineteenth century of a largely illiterate peasantry, deeply conservative and resistant to change, and for the most part living in conditions of extreme poverty, pointed to the social, political and economic backwardness of imperial Russia. Various attempts to educate the peasants had been made in the past, but such efforts had been undermined by the fear among the ruling class that any improvement in the conditions of the 'dark masses' might threaten its own privileges. It was commonplace for officials in Russia to speak of the 'safe ignorance' of the population, implying that any attempt to raise the educational standards of the masses would prove socially and politically dangerous.

iv) The Army

One method of keeping the 'dark masses' in check was to conscript numbers of them into the Russian armed services. The lower ranks of the army and navy were largely filled by enforced enlistment. Conscription was regularly used as a form of punishment for lawbreakers. The dread of conscription among ordinary Russians derived from their awareness that life in the army was invariably a brutalising experience. The Russian army was notorious in Europe for the severity of its discipline and the grimness of the conditions in which its soldiers lived. Special military camps had been set up in the remoter regions of the empire which operated as penal colonies rather than as training establishments. The rigours of service life had accounted for the deaths of over one million soldiers in peacetime during the reign of Nicholas I (1825–55).

It was a persistent belief that, as a large empire, Russia required a large army. Throughout the nineteenth century the imperial forces had a strength of around one and a half million men. The cost of maintaining the army and the navy accounted on average for forty-five per cent of the government's annual expenditure. This was by far the largest single item of state spending, and, when compared with the four per cent devoted to education, shows the order of priorities set by the government.

The higher ranks of the army were the preserve of the aristocracy. Commissions were bought and sold, and there was little room for promotion on merit. This necessarily made it less effective as a fighting force, but this fact tended to remain hidden because, with the exception of the Crimean War (1854–6), Russia was not engaged in a war with a western European power for a whole century after 1815. The army's active service was essentially a matter of putting down national risings or serious disturbances within the empire or on its frontiers. There were also frequent border wars with Turkey throughout the nineteenth century, and at various times Russian forces saw action in Poland, Armenia and Persia.

v) The Bureaucracy

Ironically, it was in the area where there had been the largest attempted reform that the greatest corruption had developed. Peter I had attempted to modernise Russia by establishing a full-scale civil service aimed at maintaining central government control throughout the empire. However, by the middle of the nineteenth century many critics within Russia had begun to condemn this civil service as a corrupt bureaucracy whose nepotism and incompetence were the principal reasons for Russia's backwardness. Alexander Herzen, a leading revolutionary writer, made the following charge in 1868:

> One of the saddest consequences of Peter I's revolution was the development of the official class. An artificial, hungry, and uneducated class, capable of doing nothing but 'serving', knowing nothing apart from official forms, it is a kind of civilian priesthood, celebrating divine serv-
> 5 ice in the law-courts and the police forces, and sucking the blood of the people with thousands of greedy, unclean mouths. There, somewhere in sooty offices which we hurry through, shabby men write page after page on grey paper, and make copies on embossed paper – and persons, families, entire villages are outraged, terrified, ruined. A father is
> 10 sent to exile, a mother to prison, a son to the army – and all this breaks over their heads like thunder, unexpected and usually undeserved.[1]

This analysis provides a valuable insight. Peter I's plan to westernise Russia had been corrupted. By the middle of the nineteenth century tsarist Russia was run by a bureaucratic class which, while incompetent and unenlightened, possessed the power to control the lives of the Russian people. At local and national levels the functioning of the law, civil administration, the police and the militia was in the hands of a set of officials whose first thought was their own convenience and advantage. Against this injustice the ordinary citizen had no redress, since any challenge to the system was lost in bureaucratic procedures.

Herzen's savage attack on the system provided powerful ammunition for those in Russia who wished to ridicule and undermine the tsarist government. However, it is important to remember that Herzen was a revolutionary propagandist intent on painting the blackest picture he could of tsardom. Efforts were made in the nineteenth century to reform the administration and limit its abuses.

3 The Problem of Reform in Imperial Russia

> **KEY ISSUE** Why was it so difficult for Russia to reform itself?

Many members of the ruling class accepted that major reforms were needed for Russia to overcome its social and economic backwardness.

However, a major block in the way of reform was a basic disagreement within the governmental elite concerning Russia's true character as a nation. Since the days of Peter the Great there had been serious differences between 'Westerners' and 'Slavophiles'. The 'Westerners' believed that if Russia wished to remain a great nation it would have to adopt the best features of the political and economic systems of the advanced countries of western Europe. The 'Slavophiles' regarded western values as corrupting and urged that the nation should preserve itself as 'holy Russia', glorying in its Slav culture and its separate historical tradition.

Another barrier to planned reform was the autocratic structure of Russia itself. Change could only come from the top. There were no representative institutions, such as a parliament, with the power to alter things. The only possible source of change was the tsar. From time to time there were progressive tsars who accepted the need for reform, but it was hardly to be expected that any tsar, no matter how enlightened, would go so far as to introduce measures that might weaken his authority. The consequence was that reform in Russia tended to be sporadic, depending on the inclinations of the individual tsar, rather than a systematic programme of modernisation. It is notable that the significant periods of reform in Russia were invariably a response to some form of national crisis or humiliation. This was certainly true of the reforms introduced in Alexander II's reign (1855–81). His accession coincided with the defeat of Russia at the hands of France and Britain in the Crimean War. The shock of this reverse prompted the new tsar into a series of major changes in Russian society.

These began with the emancipation of the serfs in 1861, followed three years later by the setting up of a network of rural councils, known as the *zemstva*. These were elected bodies, but they were not genuinely democratic, since the voting regulations left them very much in the hands of the landowners and local gentry. Nonetheless, they did provide Russia with a form of representative government, no matter how limited, which offered some hope to those progressives who longed for an extension of political rights. The authorities complemented their introduction of the *zemstva* by re-emphasising the valuable role played in the countryside by the *mir*, the traditional village commune, which government officials saw as a local organisation that would provide an effective means of keeping order as well as a cheap method of collecting taxes and mortgage repayments.

In addition, a number of legal reforms were introduced with the aim of simplifying the notoriously cumbersome court procedures whose delays had led to corruption and injustice. Of even greater importance was Alexander II's relaxation of the controls over the press and the universities. Greater freedom of expression encouraged the development of an intelligentsia, which is best defined not as a single class, but as a cross-section of the educated and more enlightened members of Russian society.

Alexander II was not a supporter of reform simply for its own sake. He saw it as a way of lessening opposition to the tsarist system. He said that his intention was to introduce reform from above in order to prevent revolution from below. His hope was that his reforms would attract the intelligentsia to side of tsardom as natural allies. The early signs were that he had succeeded. The measures of the 1860s, Emancipation and the granting of greater press and university freedoms, were greeted with enthusiasm. The intelligentsia welcomed the reforms as the basis of a genuine restructuring of Russian politics and society. However, no matter how progressive Alexander II may have appeared, he was still an autocrat. It was unthinkable that he would continue with a process that might compromise his power as tsar. Fearful that he had gone too far, he had largely abandoned his reformist policies by the 1870s. Many of the intelligentsia felt betrayed. Despairing of tsardom as a force for change, a significant number of them turned to thoughts of revolution.

Summary Diagram
Summary of Imperial Russia

INSTITUTIONS

Autocratic government

Corrupt bureaucracy

Conservative Church

Oppressive army

THE ECONOMY

Limited industrial growth

Backward agriculture

80% peasant population

Inadequate communications

POLITICS

No parliament

State censorship

Prohibition on political parties

An embittered intelligentsia

Underground revolutionary groups

Reference

1   Alexander Herzen, *My Past and Thoughts*, 1868

Working on Chapter I

The purpose of this chapter was to introduce the basic features of imperial Russia. In studying this 'background' material your aim should be to gain a broad rather than a detailed grasp of the main characteristics of the tsarist system. The key question that links the material is why imperial Russia had not modernised by the late nineteenth century. If you use the summary chart you will be reminded of the key features of the tsarist structure. Write a brief definition of the points as they appear in the three boxes. This will put you in a good position to re-read the final section which introduces some of the main explanations of why it was so difficult to achieve reform in tsarist Russia. Since this is major theme throughout this book make sure you have grasped the explanations. As always, the best way to test this is to write them down in your own words. Guidance on deeper analysis will be introduced in the chapters that follow.

2 Development and Reform 1881–1914

POINTS TO CONSIDER

This chapter builds on the knowledge you will have gained about the structure and character of Russia from your reading of chapter 1. Its four main sections deal with the basic problem of whether Russia could reform itself sufficiently to be able to compete with the major nations of western Europe. This is often referred to as Russia's period of crisis. Could it modernise itself? Section 1 describes 'the reaction', the period of repression under Alexander III. Section 2 examines the vitally important programme of economic reforms introduced in the 1890s by Witte in his attempt to modernise Russia. Section 3 looks at the agricultural reforms attempted by Stolypin in the first decade of the century. Your aim should be to gain a sound grasp of the basic problems that confronted Russia in this period. Section 4 introduces a new theme – foreign policy. This is a particularly important section as it deals with the events that led to Russia's momentous decision to go to war in 1914.

KEY DATES

1881	Alexander II assassinated by 'the People's Will'. This led to the introduction of the repressive 'temporary laws'. League of the Three Emperors formed between Russia, Germany and Austria-Hungary.
1881–95	Pobedonostsev presided over 'the Reaction', a period of severe political repression.
1885	New strict criminal code introduced.
1887	University Statute restricted academic freedoms. Re-insurance Treaty signed between Russia and Germany.
1890	*Zemstva* Act set up a network of rural councils.
1891–1902	Construction of the Trans-Siberian Railway.
1893–1903	Under Sergei Witte's leadership Russia experienced 'the great spurt' in industrial production.
1894	Accession of Nicholas II, who was to be the last tsar.
1904–5	Russo-Japanese War saw the humiliating defeat of Russia.
1905	1905 Revolution broke out.
1906	Witte dismissed as chief minister. Stolypin as chief minister embarked on a combined policy of political repression and agrarian reform.
1907	Triple Entente between France, Russia and Britain.
1908	Annexation of Bosnia-Herzegovina by Austria–Hungary. Increased tension in the Balkans.
1911	Assassination of Stolypin.
1912–13	Balkan Wars caused further Russo-Austrian tension.
1914	Russia went to war against Germany and Austria-Hungary.

1 'The Reaction'

> **KEY ISSUE**
> How far did the reaction under Alexander indicate the short-sightedness of the tsarist government?

The reign of Tsar Alexander III (1881–94) could hardly have begun in worse circumstances. The new tsar came to the throne prematurely after his father had been blown to pieces by a terrorist bomb. The assassination was the work of 'The People's Will', a group of disaffected members of the intelligentsia who reacted against Alexander II's apparent abandonment of his earlier liberalising policies (see page 12). The new tsar's response was predictable. Following the execution of five of the assassins, he turned his back on reform altogether and introduced a series of repressive measures that became known as 'the Reaction'.

> **Key measures of the Reaction**
>
> *The Statute of State Security, 1881*
> – special government-controlled courts were set up, which operated outside the existing legal system.
> – judges, magistrates and officials who were sympathetic towards liberal ideas were removed from office.
> – the powers of the *Okhrana*, the tsarist secret police, were extended, and censorship of the press was tightened.
> At its introduction in 1881, this Statute was described as a temporary measure brought in to deal with an emergency, but in essentials it remained in place until 1917. Lenin described it as 'the *de facto* constitution of Russia'. Under its terms further repression was introduced.
>
> *The University Statute, 1887*
> brought the universities under strict government control.
>
> *The Zemstva Act, 1890*
> decreased the independence of the local councils and empowered government officials to interfere in their decision-making.

a) Russification

These restrictive measures were accompanied by a deliberate policy of 'Russification'. This was an attempt by Alexander III's government to restrict the influence of the national minorities within the Russian empire. Russian was declared to be the official first language, thereby extending the traditional policy of making it the form in which law and government were conducted throughout the empire.

The effect of this was to give officials everywhere a vested interest in maintaining the dominance of Russian values at the expense of the other national cultures. Discrimination against non-Russians, which had previously been a hidden feature of Russian public life, became more open and vindictive in the 1890s. State interference in national forms of administration, education and religion became systematic. The nationalities that suffered most from the discrimination of these years were the Baltic Germans, the Poles, the Finns, the Armenians and the Ukrainians.

Particular victims of 'Russification' were the Jews. Over six hundred new measures were introduced, imposing severe social, political and economic restrictions on the Jewish population. The Jews, the majority of whom lived in distinct districts or 'ghettos', were convenient and easily identifiable scapegoats who could be blamed for Russia's difficulties. Anti-Semitism was deeply ingrained in tsarist Russia. Pogroms – fierce persecutions which often involved the wounding and killing of Jews and the destruction of their property – had long been a disfiguring feature of Russian history. A group of ultra-conservative Russian nationalists, known as the 'Black Hundreds', were notorious for their attacks upon Jews. During the reigns of Alexander III and Nicholas II the number of pogroms increased sharply. Until recently it was thought that this was proof of the tsars' active encouragement of the terrorising of the Jews. However, study of the Okhrana archives now shows that the pogroms were locally, not centrally, organised blood-lettings.

With hindsight, the tsarist policy of Russification can be seen as remarkably ill-judged. At a critical stage in its development, when cohesion and unity were needed, Russia chose to treat half its population as inferiors or potential enemies. The persecution of the Jews was especially crass. It alienated the great mass of the five million Jews in the Russian population, large numbers of whom fled in desperation to western Europe and North America, carrying with them a deep hatred of tsardom. Those who could not escape stayed to form a large and disaffected community within the empire. It was no coincidence that the 1890s witnessed a large influx of Jews into the various revolutionary movements in Russia. In 1897, Jews formed their own revolutionary 'Bund' or union.

b) The role of Pobedonostsev

The person most closely associated with the anti-Semitic policies of this period was Konstantin Pobedonostsev, chief minister in the Russian government from 1881 to 1905 and Procurator (lay head) of the Synod, the governing body of the Russian Orthodox Church. An arch-conservative by instinct and upbringing, he developed a deep distaste for all forms of liberalism and democracy. He dismissed the idea of representative government as 'the great lie of our time'. To his mind autocracy was the only possible government for imperial Russia. As personal tutor to Alexander III and Nicholas II, he played a major part in shaping the reactionary attitudes of the last two tsars. Known as 'the Grand Inquisitor' because of his repressive policies, Pobedonostsev personified the obstructions in the way of Russia's necessary political and social reform.

One of the ironies of this period was that 'the Reaction', associated with Alexander III and Pobedonostsev, coincided with a time of remarkable economic growth. It is this fact that gives added weight to the argument that in the late nineteenth and early twentieth centuries the tsarist government threw away its last chance of survival. At a critical phase, when economic developments seemed to offer a chance for Russia to modernise herself, tsardom showed a fatal resistance to change.

2 Reform

> **KEY ISSUE**
> Why did the reforms of the period prove of only limited success in modernising Russia?

a) Witte and Economic Reform

In the 1890s, Russia experienced industrial expansion on a scale that has attracted such descriptions as the 'great spurt'. A major factor in this striking development was the rapid increase in the output of coal in the Ukraine and of oil in the Caucasus. Economic historians are agreed that, although this sudden acceleration was initiated by private enterprise, it was sustained by deliberate government policy. The tsarist government's motives were military rather than economic. It is true that the capitalists (financiers and factory owners) did well out of the spurt, but it was not the government's intention to create a new capitalist class. The tsar and his ministers viewed industrialisation as a means of improving the military strength of the Russian empire.

The outstanding individual involved in this development was Sergei Witte. As minister of finance from 1893 to 1903, he set himself the huge task of modernising the Russian economy to a level comparable with the advanced nations of the west. To help bring this about, he invited large numbers of foreign experts and workers to Russia to advise on industrial planning and techniques. Engineers and managers from France, Belgium, Britain, Germany and Sweden played a vital role in Russia's 'great spurt'. It was Witte's belief that modernisation could be achieved only through state capitalism – that is, through the effective use of state power to direct and control the economy. He was impressed by the results of the industrial revolutions in western Europe and the USA, and argued that Russia could modernise rapidly and effectively by planning along the same lines. He admitted that, given the backwardness of Russia, this presented particular difficulties:

1 The economic relations of Russia to western Europe are fully comparable to the relations of colonial countries with their metropolises [mother countries]. The latter consider their colonies as advantageous markets in which they can freely sell the products of their
5 labour and of their industry, and from which they can draw with a powerful hand the raw materials necessary for them. Russia was, and to a certain extent still is, such a hospitable colony for all industrially developed states, generously providing them with the cheap products of her soil and buying dearly the products of their labour. But there
10 is a radical difference between Russia and a colony: Russia is an independent and strong power. She has the right and the strength not to want to be the handmaiden of states which are more developed economically.

In Witte's judgement, Russia's greatest need was capital for industrial investment. To raise this, he adopted a number of interlocking policies. He negotiated large loans and investments from abroad, while imposing heavy taxes and high interest rates at home. At the same time as he encouraged the inflow of foreign capital, Witte limited the import of foreign goods. Protective tariffs were set up as a means of safeguarding Russia's young domestic industries. In 1897 the Russian currency was put on the gold standard. The hope was that giving the rouble a fixed gold content would create a stable currency and so encourage international investment in Russia. The aim was largely successful but it penalised the domestic consumer since the higher-value rouble raised prices for goods already made scarce by tariff restrictions.

Much of the foreign capital that Witte was successful in raising was directly invested in railways. It was his conviction that the expansion of the railway system was the essential basis on which the modernisation of the Russian economy depended. His enthusiasm was an important factor in the extraordinary increase in lines and rolling stock that occurred between 1880 and 1914. It would not be an exaggeration to describe this as a transport revolution.

The growth of Russian railways (in miles of track)
1881 ++++++ 13,270
1891 ++++++++++++ 19,510
1900 ++++++++++++++++++++++ 33,270
1913 ++++++++++++++++++++++++++++++ 43,850

Witte's special prestige project was the Trans-Siberian Railway, which was constructed between 1891 and 1902. The line stretched for 3,750 miles from Moscow to Vladivostok (see the map on page 4) and was intended to connect the remoter regions of the central and eastern empire with the industrial west, thus encouraging the internal migration of workers to the areas where they were most needed. However, it promised more than it delivered. Sections of it were still incomplete in 1914 and it did not greatly improve east–west migration. The Trans-Siberian Railway proved more impressive as a symbol of Russian enterprise than as a project of real economic value.

One of Witte's main hopes was that the major improvements in transport would boost exports and foreign trade. The trade figures suggest that his hopes were largely fulfilled.

The Russian economy: annual production (in millions of tons)

	Coal	Pig iron	Oil	Grain (European Russia only)
1880	3.2	0.42	0.5	34
1890	5.9	0.89	3.9	36
1900	16.1	2.66	10.2	56
1910	26.8	2.99	9.4	74
1913	35.4	4.12	9.1	90
1916	33.8	3.72	9.7	64

Industrial output in the Russian Empire (base unit of 100 in 1900)

1900	100	1909	122.5
1904	109.5	1911	149.7
1905	98.2	1912	153.2
1906	111.7	1913	163.6

These figures of increased production are less impressive when it is remembered that Russia was experiencing a massive growth in population. Production per head of population was less striking than the aggregate figures.

Population of imperial Russia 1885–1913

	1885	1897	1913
European Russia	81,725,200	93,442,900	121,780,000
Caucasus	7,284,500	9,289,400	12,717,200
Siberia	4,313,700	5,758,800	9,894,500
Steppes and Urals	1,588,500	2,465,700	3,929,500
Central Asia	3,738,600	5,281,000	7,106,000
Russia	98,650,500	116,237,800	155,427,200

Growth of population in Russia's two main cities		
	St Petersburg	Moscow
1881	928,000	753,500
1890	1,033,600	1,038,600
1897	1,264,700	1,174,000
1900	1,439,600	1,345,000
1910	1,905,600	1,617,700
1914	2,217,500	1,762,700

Nevertheless, Russia was enjoying real economic expansion. Its industrial growth compared very favourably with other European countries.

Growth in national product 1898–1913		
Italy – 82.7%	Austria – 79%	Britain – 40%
Germany– 84.2%	France – 59.6%	Russia – 96.8%

There is little question that Witte's policies had a major impact on the expansion of the Russian economy, but doubts have been expressed about whether the result was wholly beneficial. His critics have argued that he made Russia too dependent on foreign loans and investments, that in giving priority to heavy industry he neglected vital areas such as light engineering, and that he paid no attention to Russia's agricultural needs.

However, any criticism of Witte should be balanced by reference to the problems he faced. The demands of the military often interfered with his plans for railway construction and the siting of industry. Moreover, his freedom of action was restricted by the resistance to change which characterised the court and the government he served. The main purpose of his economic policies was to protect tsardom against the disruptive elements in Russian society, but ironically he was distrusted by the royal court. In 1906, shortly after he had successfully negotiated a substantial loan from France, the tsar obliged him to resign. Witte faced the tragic dilemma that confronted any minister who sought to modernise tsarist Russia; he was regarded with suspicion by the representatives of the very system he was trying to save.

The improvement of the Russian economy in the 1890s was not simply the result of the work of Witte. It was part of a worldwide industrial boom. However, by the turn of the century the boom had ended and a serious international trade recession had set in. The consequences for Russia were especially serious. The industrial spurt of the last two decades of the century had led to a very rapid increase of population in the towns and cities. This increase had not been organised or supervised; the resources and facilities for accommodating the influx of workers were wholly inadequate. The result was acute over-crowding. Initially, the peasants who had left the land to take work in the urban factories accepted their grim conditions because of the considerably higher wages they were receiving. But when boom turned to recession there was widespread unemployment. The authorities in the towns and cities found themselves facing large numbers of rootless and disaffected workers who had had their expectations of a better life raised, only to be dashed by harsh economic realities. The regular presence of thousands of embittered workers on the streets of St Petersburg and Moscow played an important part in the growth of serious social unrest in Russia between 1900 and 1917.

The recession did not prove permanent. The period from 1908 to 1914 was one of overall recovery for the Russian economy, as the following figures indicate:

	1908	1914
State revenues (in roubles)	2 billion	4 billion
Number of banks	1,146	2,393
Number of factories	22,600	24,900
Number of workers	2,500,000	2,900,000
(the overall industrial growth-rate between 1908 and 1914 was 8.5%)		

Against the bright picture painted by these figures has to be set the darker aspect. In general terms the workers did not gain from the industrial and financial expansion. The absence of effective trade unions and the lack of adequate legal protection left the workforce very much at the mercy of the employers. Little of the greater amount of money in circulation reached the pockets of the workers. Although the rate of inflation rose by 40 per cent between 1908 and 1914, the average industrial wage rose from 245 to only 264 roubles per month in the same period. Of course, a national average does not tell the whole story. Some workers did relatively better than others – for example, wages were a third higher in St Petersburg than in Moscow. Nonetheless, the strike statistics compiled by the Ministry of Trade showed the scale of the industrial unrest.

Number of strikes	
1905	13,995
1908	892
1910	222
1911	466
1912	2,032
1913	2,404
1914	3,574

The question of how strong the Russian economy actually was in 1914 remains a matter of lively debate among historians. There are those who suggest that until the war came Russia was in the process of developing into a modern industrial state. They cite figures showing increased industrial production, growth of the labour force, and expansion of foreign investment. Other historians, while accepting these figures, argue that, compared to developments in other countries, Russian growth was too limited to provide a genuine industrial base. They further stress that in 1914 about four-fifths of the population were still peasants, a fact which would seem to discredit any claim that there had been significant industrial development. In the end, no definitive answer can be given to the question as to how the economy would have developed had the war and the Revolution not intervened. The comment of Alex Nove, the outstanding western authority on the Russian economy, is particularly telling:

> 1 The question of whether Russia would have become a modern industrial state but for the war and the revolution is in essence a meaningless one. One may say that statistically the answer is in the affirmative. If the growth rates characteristic of the period 1890–1913 for industry
> 5 and agriculture were simply projected over the succeeding 50 years, no doubt citizens would be leading a reasonable existence ... However, this assumes ... that the imperial authorities would have successfully made the adjustment necessary to govern in an orderly manner a rapidly developing and changing society. But there must surely be a limit to
> 10 the game of what-might-have-been.[1]

b) Stolypin and Land Reform

Peter Stolypin was appointed president of the Council of Ministers in the aftermath of the 1905 Revolution (see page 45). Like Witte before him, he was dedicated to strengthening tsardom in a time of crisis. He was a political conservative, whose attitude was clearly expressed in the coercive measures he introduced between 1906 and 1911. He declared his guiding principle to be 'suppression first and then, and only then, reform'. However, he also judged that, where possible, reform should be introduced as a way of reducing the social bitterness that produced opposition. It was in this spirit that he approached the agrarian problem in Russia. It is helpful to regard the work of Witte and Stolypin as complementary, Witte being mainly concerned with the development of industry, Stolypin with the development of agriculture. This is not to suggest that the two men co-operated in a common policy. Witte was deeply jealous of Stolypin. Nevertheless, they did share a basic objective – the preservation of the tsarist system. Indeed, it is sometimes suggested that the reforms they introduced represented the last hope that tsardom could save itself by its own efforts. Had the tsarist government and bureaucracy been willing to support Witte and Stolypin in their efforts to modernise the Russian economy, this might have prevented the build-up of the social and political tensions which culminated in the 1917 Revolution.

Stolypin appreciated that industrial progress could not of itself solve Russia's most pressing need – how to feed the nation's rapidly growing numbers. The marked increase in population that occurred in the late nineteenth century had resulted in land shortage and rural over-population. This 'rural crisis' was deepened by a series of bad harvests; the years 1891 and 1897 witnessed severe famines. The government's land policies following the emancipation of the serfs in 1861 had not helped. The scheme under which state mortgages were advanced to the emancipated serfs to enable them to buy their properties had not created the system of stable land tenure that the government had anticipated. The high price of land, which led to heavy mortgage repayments being undertaken, had impoverished the peasantry. Their sense of insecurity both inhibited them from being efficient food-producers and made them a dangerous social force. One of the reasons why the peasants joined the Revolution in 1905 was their fear that the government was about to repossess the land of the mortgage-holders who had defaulted on their payments. When the government came to understand this fear, it bought off the peasants by announcing that the outstanding repayments would be cancelled (see page 48).

Stolypin planned to build upon this successful 'de-revolutionising' of the peasantry. In 1906 and 1907 he introduced measures which allowed the individual peasant to opt out of the *mir*. The position of the independent householder was promoted. Peasants were encouraged to replace the antiquated strip system with separate blocks of land, based on the pattern that existed in western Europe. A special Land Bank was established to allocate funds to assist the independent peasant to buy his land. Stolypin defined his policy as 'the wager on the strong'. His aim was to create a stratum of prosperous, efficient peasants whose new wealth would turn them into natural supporters and allies of the tsarist system. This would effectively decapitate the peasantry as a revolutionary movement. He complemented his land reform policy by supporting schemes for large-scale voluntary resettlement of the peasants. The aim was to populate the empire's remoter areas, such as Siberia, and bring them into productive agricultural use.

Even in advanced economies land reforms take time to work. Stolypin was well aware that, in a country as relatively backward as Russia, reforms would take even longer to become effective. He spoke of needing twenty years for his 'wager on the strong' to show dividends. In the event, his assassination in 1911 allowed him personally only five, and the war in 1914 allowed Russia only eight. However, there is doubt whether, even without the intrusion of murder and war, his peasant policy would have succeeded. The deep conservatism of the Russian peasants made them slow to respond. In 1914 the strip system still prevailed; only about 10 per cent of the land had been consolidated into farms. The peasants were reluctant to leave the security of the commune for the uncertainty of individual farming. Furthermore, by 1913 the Ministry of Agriculture had itself begun to show signs of losing confidence in the policy.

Number of peasant households becoming independent

(out of an estimated total of 10–12 million households)

1907	48,271	1911	145,567
1908	508,344	1912	122,314
1909	579,409	1913	134,554
1910	342,245	1914	97,877

One notable feature of Stolypin's land policy was his effective working relations with the duma. This elected assembly, which had been set up under the terms of the tsar's October Manifesto in 1905 (see page 48), had not been granted legislative powers. Nonetheless, it did provide for the first time in Russian history a forum for public discussion at national level. Stolypin chose to treat it with respect. The understanding which developed between him and the Octobrists, the largest party in the duma, allowed him to pursue his land reforms with little obstruction from the duma deputies. His success in this regard hinted at what might have been achieved in terms of co-operation between government and progressive opinion, had tsarist authorities been willing to trust their own ministers.

3 Russian Foreign Policy

> **KEY ISSUES** Why was imperial Russia defensive in its dealings with the European Powers?
> Did the Russo-Japanese War serve any genuine Russian interests?

a) Russian Objectives

The foreign policy of tsarist Russia was largely determined by the size of its empire. The protection of its many frontiers was a constant preoccupation. Three particular developments had occurred in Europe in the second half of the nineteenth century which alarmed Russia: the growth of a united Germany, the formation of the Austro-Hungarian Empire, and the continued decline of the Turkish Empire. Russia feared that the unification of Germany in 1871 had left central Europe dominated by a young and powerful nation, ambitious to expand eastwards. The process of German unification had involved the military and diplomatic defeat of Austria. Russia was concerned that Austria, which had been enlarged into the Austro-Hungarian Empire in 1867, would build on its new strength by an expansionist policy in south-east Europe. This might be encouraged by the decay of Turkey's authority over its possessions in the Balkans, where a number of aggressive national movements were challenging Turkish rule.

Russia's attitude towards Turkey was governed by two factors. One was its traditional wish, as a predominantly Slav nation, to protect the Slav Christian peoples of the Balkans from Turkish Islamic oppression. The other was a concern for its commercial interests. Of Russia's grain exports, 75 per cent (which accounted for 40 per cent of its total foreign trade) were shipped through the Straits of the Dardanelles. It was, therefore, necessary to ensure that the Straits did not come under the control of a potentially hostile power capable of interrupting the passage of Russian ships from the Black Sea into the Mediterranean.

The Dardanelles.

Russia's anxieties about the strength and intentions of the European powers led to its taking a cautious and conciliatory approach towards them. During the reigns of the last two tsars, Russia's response to the shifts and turns of European diplomacy was consistently self-protective and defensive. It was reluctant to take the diplomatic initiative, but it was willing to enter into alliances and agreements which offered a greater chance of preserving the security of its western borders and possessions. In particular, it was concerned that its traditional control over Poland should not be weakened.

Things augured well for Russia at the beginning of Alexander III's reign. In response to a proposal by Bismarck, the German Chancellor, Russia joined Austria-Hungary and Germany in the League of the Three Emperors (1881), an agreement by which each of the powers promised not to support the enemy should any of them become involved in war with a fourth country. This accord did not survive long. In the mid-1880s tension arose between Russia and Austria-Hungary over the latter's support for anti-Russian movements in Bulgaria. The Three Emperors League was not renewed. In its place, Russia and Germany signed a secret Reinsurance Treaty (1887), which recognised Russian claims in Bulgaria and promised German neutrality in the event of a Russo-Austrian war.

b) Russia and the Alliance System

Germany under Bismarck had dominated the European scene by playing upon the fears of each nation of becoming isolated in a world of alliances. However, in 1890 Bismarck was dismissed by the new German Kaiser, William II. Under its new ruler, Germany adopted a more aggressive form of diplomacy which had the effect of polarising international attitudes and led eventually to the splitting of Europe into two opposed, armed camps. William II declined to renew the Reinsurance Treaty. Instead, he showed every intention of joining with Austria in asserting German influence in the Balkans and the Near East. To avoid isolation, Russia turned first to France. These two countries had not been on good terms, but a common fear of German aggression now outweighed their traditional dislike of each other. The Franco-Russian Convention, signed in 1892, committed each partner to the military support of the other should it go to war with Germany. Their economic co-operation also brought them closer. France was the major foreign investor in Russia during the industrial take-off of the 1880s and 1890s.

The original alliance between France and Russia expanded into a Triple Entente, with the inclusion of Britain in 1907. This, too, was something of a diplomatic revolution. Anglo-Russian relations had been strained for decades. Imperial rivalries in Asia and Britain's resistance to what it regarded as Russia's attempts to dominate the eastern Mediterranean had aroused mutual animosity. Indeed, during the 1890s Britain seemed more drawn to the Triple Alliance than to France and Russia. However, by the turn of the century Germany had embarked on an expansive naval programme which Britain interpreted as a direct threat to is own security and to its empire. Britain's response was to form an understanding with Germany's major western and eastern neighbours, France and Russia. In the Anglo-French Entente of 1904, Britain and France had already agreed to abandon their old rivalry. It made diplomatic sense for Russia and Britain to do the same. Consequently, in 1907 they agreed to settle their past differences by recognising each other's legitimate interests in Afghanistan, Persia and Tibet. No precise agreement was reached regarding the matter of military co-operation in Europe but there was a broad understanding that such co-operation would follow in the event of war.

c) The Russo-Japanese War, 1904–5

What had helped prepare the way for the Anglo-Russian *rapprochement* was the Russo-Japanese War of 1904–5. This struggle arose in part from Russia's decision to pursue an expansionist policy in the Far East, both as a means of compensating for its relative decline in Europe and as a way of obtaining an ice-free port. It was also an attempt by the tsarist government to distract attention from Russia's domestic troubles by rallying the nation in a patriotic struggle. Care has to be taken over this last point. The blame for Russia's going to war against Japan has customarily been laid upon Plehve, the minister of the interior, who was reputed to have said 'We need a small, victorious war to avert a revolution'. However, recent research has shown that this verdict rests upon misinformation deliberately spread by Witte, Plehve's enemy. Richard Pipes observes:

1 It has since become known that Plehve did not want a war ... Witte himself bore a great deal of the blame for the conflict ... Witte's plans for economic penetration of the Far East ... called for a strong military presence, which was sooner or later to come into conflict with the
5 imperial ambitions of Japan.[2]

The Russians looked on Japan as a semi-feudal state, and no match for themselves. Pretexts for war were not hard to find. Territorial disputes between Russia and Japan over Korea and Manchuria had simmered for some time. In 1904, the Russian authorities deliberately rejected Japanese proposals for the settlement of the Korean question in the hope that this would excite a military response. The ruse worked: Japan opened hostilities by attacking the Russian fleet in Port Arthur.

That proved to be the only accurate calculation made by the Russian government in the whole affair. The rest was a tale of confusion and disaster. Japan was not the backward state the Russians had imagined. Under the Emperor Meiji (1869–1914) it had embarked upon a series of sweeping reforms aimed at rapid modernisation along Western lines. The Japanese army and navy were far better prepared and equipped than the Russian forces and won a series of major victories. After a long siege, Port Arthur fell to Japan in January 1905. The following month, the Japanese forced home their advantage by driving the Russians out of the key Manchurian town of Mukden. The final catastrophe for Russia came at sea. The Russian Baltic fleet, dispatched to the Far East in 1904, took eight months to reach its destination, only to be blown out of the water immediately on its arrival by the Japanese fleet at Tsushima in May 1905. Such defeats obliged the tsarist government to make peace. In the Treaty of Portsmouth, Russia agreed to withdraw its remaining forces from Manchuria and accepted Japanese control of Korea and Port Arthur.

Russia lost the war not because its troops fought badly, but because its military commanders had not prepared effectively. They understood neither the enemy they were fighting nor the territory in which the struggle took place. Their unimaginative strategy allowed the Japanese to outmanoeuvre the Russian forces. The distance over which men and materials had to be transported from western Russia made it impossible to provide adequate reinforcements and supplies. The Trans-Siberian Railway, still incomplete in a number of sections, proved of little value. Russia's defeat at the hands of a small, supposedly inferior, Asian country was a national humiliation. Within Russia, the incompetence of the government, which the war glaringly revealed, excited the social unrest which it had been specifically designed to dampen.

d) The Balkans

Its defeat in Asia made Russia keener still to form protective alliances with friendly European powers. The area of most immediate concern was the Balkans. The revolt of the 'Young Turks' against the sultanate in 1908 marked a further stage in the collapse of Turkish power. Despite the wrangling that went on between their various ambassadors in the Balkan states, Russia and Austria-Hungary seemed genuinely willing to co-operate at government level. In 1908, the Russian foreign minister, Izvolski, was urged by his Austrian counterpart, Aehrenthal, to accept the annexation of Bosnia and Herzegovina by Austria-Hungary as a means of creating greater stability in the Balkan region. Izvolski agreed to the proposal in return for Austria-Hungary's promise that it would acknowledge Russia's unfettered right to the use of the Straits, and would persuade the other European powers to do the same. Austria-Hungary duly announced the takeover of Bosnia and Herzegovina, but then failed to make any effort to encourage the international recognition of Russian rights in the Straits.

From this time onwards, relations between Russia and Austria-

Hungary steadily deteriorated. A key issue dividing them was the position of Serbia. Bosnia contained many Serbs and its annexation by Austria-Hungary in 1908 aroused fierce Serbian nationalism. Russia, viewing itself as the special defender of Serbia and its predominantly Slav people, backed it in demanding compensation and the calling of an international conference to consider the annexation. Germany sided aggressively with Austria-Hungary and warned Russia not to interfere. The crisis threatened for a time to spill into war. However, in 1909 none of the countries involved felt ready to fight. Russia backed off from an open confrontation, while at the same time letting it be known internationally that it regarded Germany and Austria-Hungary as the aggressors.

Between 1909 and 1914 Russia continued to involve itself in the complexities of Balkan nationalist politics. Its aim was to prevent Austria-Hungary from gaining a major advantage in the region. The tactic was to try to persuade the various nationalities in the region to form a coalition against Austria-Hungary. Russia had some success in this. Balkan nationalism led to a series of conflicts, known collectively as the Balkan Wars (1912–13). These were a confused mixture of anti-Turkish uprisings and squabbles between the Balkan states themselves over the division of the territories they had won from the Turks. On balance, the outcome of these wars favoured Russian rather than Austro-Hungarian interests. Serbia had been doubled in size and felt herself more closely tied to Russia as an ally and protector, while Austria-Hungary's client states, Romania and Bulgaria, had not done well in the wars. However, such gains as Russia had made were marginal. The international issues relating to Turkish decline and Balkan nationalism had not been resolved. The events of 1914 were to show how vulnerable imperial Russia's status and security actually were.

4 Conclusion

> **KEY ISSUE** Had the period 1881–1914 been a race against time for the tsarist system?

Between 1881 and 1914 Russia took a number of significant steps towards modernisation. Serious efforts were made to reform the economy, and progressive agricultural changes were introduced. Important adjustments were made in foreign policy in an effort to end old antagonisms and provide greater national security. These were not inconsiderable achievements. Foreign observers commented favourably on the advances that had been made.

However, despite some limited modifications of tsarist authority during the period, Russia in 1914 was still essentially an absolutist state. A fundamental question remained unanswered in 1914. Was

Russian capable or, indeed, willing to adopt the political and social changes necessary for it to become a modern state comparable with those of western Europe? This problem, which is often referred to as the 'the tsarist crisis' or 'the institutional crisis', had been neatly summarised in question form by Robert Service, the outstanding Lenin scholar:

 1 It was a race against time. Would the tsarist system sustain its energy
    and authority for a sufficient period to modernise society and the econ-
    omy? Would the revolutionaries accommodate themselves to the
    changing realities and avoid the excesses of violent politics? And would
 5 the tsarist system make concessions to bring this about?[3]

References

1   Alex Nove, *An Economic History of the USSR* (Penguin, 1973) p.17
2   Richard Pipes, *The Russian Revolution 1899–1919* (Collins Harvill, 1990) p.12
3   Robert Service, *Lenin A Biography* (Macmillan, 2000) p.4

Working on Chapter 2

The chapter takes a broadly chronological approach in its analysis of the principal features of government repression and reform during this period. You are advised to follow the same pattern when analysing the three key areas. Use the first column of the summary to guide you as to the main points of the reaction. Against each of the headings write a brief comment to indicate that you understand its significance. Contrast these with reforms listed in the centre column. This will test your understanding of both movements and of the tension between them and of the difficulties that confronted reformers. The third area of analysis, foreign policy, is distinct from the other two but by using the third column in a similar way you should be able to highlight the principal developments.

Source-based questions on Chapter 2

To familiarise yourself with the type of question you are likely to be asked, study the following questions:

The economic reforms of Witte and Stolypin
Study Witte's analysis on page 19 and the tables of statistics on pages 19–22.

 1. **Comprehension questions**, the type that tests your basic understanding of the sources. Examples are:

Summary Diagram

Reaction	Reform	Foreign Affairs
Pobedonostev 1881–1905		3 Emperors League 1881
Statute of State Security 1881	Witte 1893–1906 the great spurt	
	Population growth	The German issue
University Statute 1887	Foreign capital	
	Investment	
Zemstva Statute 1890	Railways	Austro-Hungarian-Turkish question
	Regional development	
Russification	industrial output	Franco-Russian Convention 1892
Anti-Jewish Laws		
Pogroms The Black 100s	October Manifesto 1905	Russo-Japanese War 1904–05
	Dumas 1906–14	
The Stolypin repression 1906–11	The Stolypin reforms 1906–11: Debt cancellation Land bank The wager on the strong	Triple Entente 1907
		The Balkan crises 1908–14

Why, according to Witte's analysis, had Russia's economic growth lagged behind that of the countries of western Europe? (5 marks)

What can you learn from the statistics about the improvement in Russia's industry and agriculture that resulted from the policies of Witte and Stolypin? (8 marks)

2. **Stimulus questions**, the type that ask you to draw on your own knowledge to explain the meaning of a key concept or the role and/or importance of a key individual or institution. A typical question might be: Using your own knowledge, explain why Witte and Stolypin were unable to achieve their complete economic objectives. (10 marks)

3. **Cross referencing questions**, the type that ask you to compare the content of two or more sources and reaching a conclusion based on the comparison. A typical question might be:

How far is the claim by Witte that Russia was an economic colony of the more advanced states supported by the statistics on pages 20–21? (12 marks)

4. **Source evaluation questions**, the type that asks you to judge the usefulness and/or reliability of one or two primary sources. A typical question might be:

    How valuable are these sources to the historian who is studying the strength of the tsarist economy in 1914? (12 marks)

5. **Lead-out questions**, the type that asks you to use one or two of the sources and your own knowledge to provide a historical explanation. A typical question might be:

    Explain how these sources help to explain why Witte and Stolypin met resistance to their policies from the tsarist government. (15 marks)

3 Opposition to Tsardom 1881–1914

POINTS TO CONSIDER

This chapter takes as its main theme the growth of resistance to the tsarist regime. It looks at the range of movements, from those which advocated moderate reform through to those which believed in destroying tsardom altogether. There is an understandable tendency among historians to concentrate on those forces which were eventually to take power in the revolution of 1917. But it is important to remember that the victory of the Bolsheviks in 1917 was not inevitable. To gain a balanced view of the period covered by this chapter you need to be familiar with the other groups and parties that offered alternative solutions to the problem of how Russia could modernise itself.

KEY DATES

1870 Birth of Vladimir Ulyanov (Lenin).
1870s Populist (Narodnik) peasant revolutionary movement developed.
1871 Populist terrorist group , 'The People's Will', was founded.
1881 Alexander II assassinated by 'The People's Will'.
1887 Lenin's elder brother executed for his involvement in a plot to murder Alexander III.
1897 Revolutionary Jewish Bund formed.
1898 All Russian Social Democratic Workers' Party (the SDs) of Marxist revolutionaries formed.
1901 Social Revolutionary Party (SRs), a development of Populism, formed under Victor Chernov
1902 Lenin published his pamphlet, *What Is To Be Done*, setting out his revolutionary programme.
1903 SDs split into Mensheviks (under Plekhanov) and Bolsheviks (under Lenin).
1905 Constitutional Democratic Party (Kadets) formed under Paul Milyukov.
Moderate reforming party, the Octobrists, led by Alexander Guchkov formed after the issuing of tsar's October Manifesto.
Soviets formed in St. Petersburg and Moscow.
1906 First Duma sat between April and June.
1907 Second Duma sat between February and June.
Third Duma began in November.
1911 Stolypin assassinated.
1912 Serious disturbances occurred in the Lena goldfields, Siberia.
Third Duma dissolved in June.
Fourth Duma began in November.

1912 First edition of the Bolshevik newspaper, *Pravda*, published.
1914 Fourth Duma suspended on the outbreak of war in August.

1 Introductory Survey

'The Reaction' that began under Alexander III and continued in the
reign of Nicholas II (1894–1917) oppressed, but did not destroy,
opposition to the tsarist regime. Indeed, despite greater police sur-
veillance, opposition became more organised. A number of political
parties, ranging from moderate reformers to violent revolutionaries,
came into being. The government's policies of reaction and
Russification combined to produce a situation in which many political and national groups were becoming increasingly frustrated by
the mixture of coercion and incompetence that characterised the
tsarist system. The rapid industrial growth in the 1890s had created
a special problem. It had brought to the cities large numbers of
peasants, who were attracted by the prospect of relatively well-paid
factory work. When a depression followed in the first decade of the
twentieth century it left many of these new industrial workers unem-
ployed and angry. Their bitterness made them a serious threat to
public order.

The government attempted to meet the problem by diverting
attention away from domestic issues with a war against Japan in the
Far East (see page 28). The aim was to unite the nation, but the
reverse happened. Russia's humiliating military defeat in 1905 was
blamed directly on the government's inept handling of the war. It was
no coincidence that workers, peasants and middle-class liberals joined
together in the year of Russia's defeat in a series of anti-government
protests, which were serious enough to merit the description 'the
1905 Revolution'.

The disturbances obliged Nicholas II to make a number of political concessions. In his October Manifesto, he reluctantly gave in to
the demand for the formation of a duma. But this did not mark a liberalising of the regime, as was soon illustrated by the ferocity of the
political repression that followed once the disorder had been ended.
The government, led by Stolypin as chief minister from 1906 to 1911,
was ruthless in crushing opposition. But the strikes and disturbances
continued despite the repression. By 1914, many reformists had
become so disillusioned with the failure of the 1905 Revolution to
lead to real advance that they had begun to consider violence as the
only means by which to change the oppressive yet incapable tsarist
regime.

Until the issuing of the October Manifesto in 1905, political parties
were illegal in Russia. This had not actually prevented their formation
but it had stifled their development as genuinely democratic bodies.
Denied legal recognition, they often resorted to extreme methods in

order to spread their ideas. As a result, during the brief period of their permitted existence from 1905 to 1921, the Russian political parties proved generally to be highly suspicious and intolerant of each other. This made co-operation and collective action difficult to organise and sustain. Four main groups opposed to tsardom can be identified: the Populists, the Social Revolutionaries, the Social Democrats, and the liberals.

2 The Populists (*Narodniks*)

> **KEY ISSUE** How did populism help to stimulate a revolutionary atmosphere in late imperial Russia?

Populism as a revolutionary movement dated from the 1870s. It regarded the future of Russia as being in the hands of the peasants who made up the overwhelming mass of the population. The Populists or *Narodniks* (from the Russian word for 'the people') looked to the peasants to take the lead in the transforming of Russia, beginning with the overthrow of the tsarist system itself. As with all the significant political movements that came into being in this period, the Populist leaders were drawn, not from the peasants, but from the middle and upper classes. The Populists regarded it as their duty to educate the uninformed peasantry into an awareness of its revolutionary potential. This involved 'going to the people', a policy by which the educated Populists went from the universities into the countryside to live for a period with the peasants in an attempt to incite them to revolution.

The scheme met with little success. The peasants were largely unmoved by the revolutionary socialist message preached to them. In desperation, some Populists turned to terrorism, which they defined euphemistically as 'the propaganda of the deed', as the only way of achieving their aims. In 1879, a group calling itself 'The People's Will' was founded with the declared intention of murdering members of the ruling class. This group, which was reckoned to be no more than 400 strong, gained notoriety two years later with its assassination of Alexander II. However, this act weakened rather than strengthened the Populist movement. The murder of a tsar who had initiated many reforms seemed to discredit the idea of reform itself and so justified the repression imposed in the aftermath of the assassination.

The importance of Populism lay in its methods rather than in its ideas. Its concept of a peasant-based revolution appeared unrealistic, given the political inertia of the Russian peasantry. What was lasting about Populism was the part it played in establishing a revolutionary tradition. All the revolutionaries in Russia after 1870 were influenced, if not inspired, by the example of the Populist challenge to tsardom.

3 The Social Revolutionaries (SRs)

> **KEY ISSUE** What range of opinion in Russia did the SRs represent?

The Social Revolutionary Party grew directly out of the Populist movement. The quickening of interest in political and social issues which accompanied the economic spurt of the 1890s was viewed by Populists as an opportunity to gain recruits for their revolutionary cause. They attempted to broaden their basis of appeal in order to attract the rapidly growing urban workforce to their revolutionary programme. The intention was to widen the concept of the 'people', so that it encompassed all those who wanted the destruction of the tsarist system. An important figure in this reshaping of Populist strategy was Victor Chernov, who played a major part in the formation of the Social Revolutionary Party in 1901 and became its leader. He was a member of the intelligentsia, and sought to provide a firmer theoretical base for Populism than its previous passionate but vague ideas had produced. However, as with all the revolutionary groups in tsarist Russia, the SRs were weakened by disagreements among themselves. Lev Trotsky described them in these terms:

> 1   [They were] formed at the beginning of the century from a fusion of several tendencies of the *Narodniks*. Representing the wavering interests of the small peasant proprietor, the party soon split into a group of Left Social Revolutionaries, anarchist in their leanings, and the
> 5   Right Social Revolutionaries.[1]

In distinguishing between the left and the right elements, Trotsky was referring to the division of the SR Party into anarchists and revolutionaries. The former were the faction who wanted to continue the policy of terrorism inherited from 'The People's Will'. The latter were the more moderate element, who, while believing in revolution as their ultimate goal, were prepared to co-operate with other parties in working for an immediate improvement in the conditions of the workers and peasants. Between 1901 and 1905, it was the terrorist faction that dominated. During those years the SRs were responsible for over 2,000 political assassinations, including Plehve, the interior minister, and the tsar's uncle, the Grand Duke Sergei. These were spectacular successes but they did little to forge the desired link with the urban workers.

The 1905 Revolution brought more gains to the liberals than to the revolutionaries (see page 49). One effect of this on the SRs was that the more moderate element gained greater influence over party policy. This began to show dividends. From 1906, the SRs experienced a growing support from the professional classes, from the trade unions (which had been legalised under the October Manifesto), and from the All-Russian Union of Peasants, which had been set up in 1905. At its first congress in 1906, the SR Party committed itself to 'revolutionary socialism' and gave a special pledge to the peasants that it would end 'the bourgeois principle of private ownership by returning the land to those who worked it'. It was their land policy which largely explains why the SRs remained the most popular party with the peasants. However, at the time, the congress decisions brought disruption rather than unity. The left wing broke away on the grounds that the party's programme ignored the industrial proletariat, while the right wing complained that congress policy was unworkable in current Russian conditions. Chernov tried to hold the factions together, but from 1906 onwards the SRs constituted a collection of radical groups rather than a genuinely co-ordinated party. Nevertheless, until they were outlawed by the Bolsheviks (see page 109) the SRs remained the party with largest popular following in Russia.

4 The Social Democrats (the SDs)

KEY ISSUE Why did Lenin develop a separate Bolshevik party within the SD?

The All-Russian Social Democratic Labour Party was formed in 1898 as a Marxist party.

Marxism

Karl Marx (1818–83), the German revolutionary, had advanced the idea that human society operated according to in-built mechanisms which could be scientifically studied and then applied. He asserted that history was a continuous series of class struggles between those who possessed economic and political power and those who did not. The form of the conflict changed according to the historical period, but the essential struggle between the 'haves' and the 'have-nots' was constant. He referred to this process of continuous class struggle as the dialectic. For revolutionaries in the nineteenth century, the most exciting aspect of Marx's analysis was his conviction that the contemporary industrial era marked the final stage of the dialectical class struggle. Human history was about to reach its culmination in the revolutionary victory of the proletariat (the industrial working class) over the bourgeoisie (the exploiting, capitalist, class).

The attraction of Marx for Russian revolutionaries is easy to understand. His ideas had been known in Russia for some time, but what gave them particular relevance was the 'great spurt' of the 1890s. This promised to create the industrial conditions in Russia which would make a successful revolution possible. The previously unfocused hopes for revolution could now be directed on the industrial working class. The first Marxist revolutionary of note in Russia was George Plekhanov. He had translated Marx's writings into Russian, and in 1883 had helped to found the first Marxist organisation in the country, the 'Group for the Emancipation of Labour'. His efforts to promote the idea of proletarian revolution had earned him the title 'the father of Russian Marxism'. Despite this, a number of the revolutionaries who had formed the SD Party in 1898 soon became impatient with Plekhanov's leadership. They found him too theoretical in his approach, and urged the adoption of more active revolutionary policies. The outstanding spokesman for this viewpoint was Vladimir Ulyanov, better known by his revolutionary pseudonym as Lenin.

V.I. LENIN

-Profile-

1870	Lenin born as Vladimir Ilyich Ulyanov to a minor aristocratic family of Jewish ancestry
1887	his brother's execution intensified Lenin's revolutionary attitude
1897	exiled to Siberia, took the name Lenin (the most famous of the 160 aliases he used as a revolutionary)
1900	joined SD party
1902	wrote *What is to be Done?*
1903	led the Bolshevik breakaway movement in the SD
1905	returned to Russia in December but played no part in the Revolution
1906–17	in exile abroad for much of this period
1917	returned to Petrograd following the February Revolution and led the Bolsheviks in a successful coup in October
1917–20	led the Bolsheviks in consolidating their hold on Russia
1918	injured in an SR attempt on his life
1921	introduced NEP to save Russia from starvation

1922–23 suffered a number of severe strokes which left him
         speechless
1924   died

Lenin had been on the tsarist authorities' list of 'dangerous persons' since he was 17. The execution of his elder brother in 1887
for his part in an attempted assassination of Alexander III had
made Lenin himself politically suspect. He lived up to his reputation. By the age of 20, his voracious reading of Marx's writings
had turned him into a committed Marxist for whom revolution
was a way of life. By the age of 30, his dedication to the cause of
revolution in Russia had led to his arrest, imprisonment, and
internal exile. Indeed, he was in exile in Siberia when the SD
Party was formed in 1898. When he returned to western Russia
two years later he set about turning the SD into a genuinely revolutionary party. With an SD colleague, Julius Martov, he
founded a party newspaper, *Iskra* (the Spark), which he used as
the chief means of putting his case to the party members. Lenin
was concerned that Plekhanov was more interested in reform
than in revolution. He was worried that the SDs were attempting
to improve the conditions of the workers (a policy referred to as
'economism'), instead of pursuing their true goal, the transformation of the workers into a revolutionary force for the overthrow of capitalism. Lenin wanted conditions to get worse, not
better. In that way the bitterness of the industrial proletariat
would increase, and so bring revolution nearer.

Although Lenin despised the moderate, reformist intelligentsia, he argued, nonetheless, that it was only from that intellectual class that the leaders of revolution in Russia could be
drawn. He set down his ideas on this theme in his pamphlet,
What is to be Done?, published in 1902. The following extract is a
key passage from it:

1   The history of every country teaches us that by its own ability the
    working class can attain only a trade-unionist self-consciousness,
    that is to say, an appreciation of the need to fight the bosses, to
    wrest from the government this or that legislative enactment for
5   the benefit of the workers. The Socialist [Communist] doctrine,
    on the other hand, is the outgrowth of those philosophical, his-
    torical and economic theories which had been developed by the
    representatives of the well to do, the intellectuals. By their social
    origin, Marx and Engels, the founders of modern scientific social-
10 ism, were themselves members of the bourgeois intelligentsia. The
    blind unfolding of the labour movement can lead only to the per-
    meation of that movement with a bourgeois ideology, because the
    unconscious growth of the labour movement takes the form of
    trade unionism, and trade unionism signifies the mental enslave-
15 ment of the workers to the bourgeoisie.

> 20 Therefore our task as Social Democrats is to oppose this blind process, to divert the labour movement from the unconscious tendency of trade unionism to march under the protective wing of the bourgeoisie and to bring it under the influence of Social Democracy instead.

Such beliefs inspired Lenin throughout his life. Orlando Figes said of him:

> 1 [T]here was no 'private Lenin' behind the public mask. He gave all of himself to politics. He rarely showed emotion, he had few intimates, and everything he ever said or wrote was intended only for the revolutionary cause. This was not a man but a political machine.
> 5 Lenin's personal life was extraordinarily dull. ... He did not smoke, he did not really drink, and apart from his affair with the beautiful Inessa Armand, he was not even interested in women. Krupskaya [his wife] called him 'Ilich', his nickname in the party, and he called her 'comrade'. She was more like his secretary than
> 10 his wife, and it was probably not bad luck that their marriage was childless.
> Lenin lived for the revolution.
>
> *From a review article by Orlando Figes in The Sunday Times, Mar 2000*

Lenin wrote *What Is To Be Done?* as an answer to the followers of Plekhanov, who were continuing to assert that success could be gained only by a broad grouping of the progressive, reformist, anti-tsarist elements in Russia. Lenin insisted that the way forward could be effectively organised only by a dedicated group of professional revolutionaries. His reference to the scientific nature of socialism was a crucial part of his argument. Revolution for Lenin was not a haphazard affair; it was part of a natural progression whose laws could be understood by scientific analysis. He considered that Marx had, indeed, already provided this understanding. What remained now was for true Marxist followers to apply the revolutionary message in Russia. This was why the workers could not be left to themselves; only through the leadership of the truly informed could the proletariat of Russia achieve victory in the class war. In the Russian context, this leadership was supplied by the revolutionary intelligentsia, which according to Lenin consisted, in effect, of himself and those Marxists who agreed with him. Only they could rescue the Russian working class and convert it to true socialism.

a) The Bolshevik–Menshevik split

The dispute between Lenin and Plekhanov came to a head during the second congress of the SD Party in 1903. Plekhanov tried to avoid confrontation, but Lenin deliberately made an issue of who had the right to membership of the Social Democratic Party. His aim was to force the SDs to choose between Plekhanov's idea of a broad-based party, open to all revolutionaries, and his own concept of a small, tightly-knit and exclusive party of professional revolutionaries. The congress was a heated affair, which often broke down into a series of slanging matches over points of procedure. A deep divide developed between Lenin and his *Iskra* co-editor, Martov. Their quarrel had as much to do with personality as with politics. Martov believed that behind Lenin's procedural tactics was a fierce determination to become dictator of the party. The following was typical of their exchanges:

1 *Martov* – The more widely the title of 'member of the party' is spread, the better. We can only rejoice if every striker, every demonstrator, is able to declare himself a party member.

   Lenin – It is better that ten real workers should not call themselves
5 party members than that one chatterbox should have the right and opportunity to be a member.

In a series of votes, the SD congress showed itself to be evenly divided between Lenin and Martov. However, after a particular set of divisions had gone in his favour, Lenin claimed that he and his supporters were the majority. This led to their being called Bolsheviks (from *bolshinstvo*, Russian for majority) while Martov's group became known as Mensheviks (from *menshinstvo*, Russian for minority).

By 1912 the Bolsheviks and Mensheviks had become two distinct and opposed Marxist parties. Lenin deliberately emphasised the difference between himself and Martov by resigning from the editorial board of *Iskra* and starting his own journal, *Vyperod* (Forward), as an instrument for Bolshevik attacks upon the Mensheviks. A Bolshevik daily paper, *Pravda* (the Truth), was first published in 1912. Initially, the main point dividing Bolsheviks and Mensheviks was simply one of procedure. However, following the split in 1903 the differences between them hardened into a set of opposed attitudes. These can be illustrated in tabulated form:

Menshevik view	**issue**	**Bolshevik view**
⬇	*Revolution*	⬇
Russia not yet ready for proletarian revolution – the bourgeois stage had to occur first		Bourgeois and proletarian stages could be telescoped into one revolution
⬇	*The Party*	⬇
a mass organisation with membership open to all revolutionaries		a tight-knit, exclusive, organisation of professional revolutionaries

	Discipline	
▼		▼
Open, democratic discussion within the party – decisions arrived at by votes of members		Authority to be exercised by the Central Committee of the party – this described as 'democratic centralism'
▼	*Strategy*	▼
Alliance with all other revolutionary and bourgeois liberal parties – support of trade unions in pursuing better wages and conditions for workers (economism)		no co-operation with other parties – economism dismissed as playing into hands of bourgeoisie – aimed to turn workers into revolutionaries

Care should be taken not to allow hindsight to exaggerate the accuracy of Lenin's judgements or the significance of his role during the pre-revolutionary years. The later success of Bolshevism in the October Revolution (see page 95) has tempted writers to overstate the importance of Lenin in the period before 1917. For example, Trotsky, who joined Lenin in 1917 after having been a Menshevik, argued in his later writings that the Bolsheviks had been systematically preparing the ground for revolution since 1903. But the fact was that during the years 1904 to 1917 Lenin was largely absent from Russia; his visits were rare and fleeting. Although he continued from exile to issue a constant stream of instructions to his followers, the Bolsheviks played only a minor role in events in Russia before 1914.

Interestingly, the Bolsheviks were not listed by the police authorities as a major challenge to the tsarist system. In the pre-1914 period the numerical strength of the Bolsheviks varied between 5,000 and 10,000; even in February 1917 it was no more than 25,000. Before 1917, the Mensheviks invariably outnumbered them. Numbers, of course, are not everything. Determination is arguably more important. Whatever the apparent lack of influence of Lenin's Bolsheviks before 1917, the fact is that when a revolutionary situation developed in 1917 it was they who proved the best prepared to seize the opportunity to take over government. That in itself testifies to the real strength of the revolutionary party Lenin had created.

5 The Liberals

> **KEY ISSUE** What had encouraged the growth of a liberal movement in tsarist Russia?

> **Liberalism**
>
> As used in Russia, the term 'liberal' described those who wanted political or social change, but who believed that it could be achieved by reforming rather than destroying the tsarist system.

The land reforms of Alexander II, which had led to the spread of the *zemstva*, had helped to create a progressive middle class in the countryside. This had been matched in the urban areas. The economic boom of the 1890s saw the rapid development of a small but ambitious class of industrialists, lawyers and financiers. It was among such social groups that liberal ideas for the modernising of Russia began to take hold. There was also often a strong national element in Russian liberalism. The national minorities viewed the liberal movement as a means of expressing their wish to be independent of Russian imperial control. Two principal liberal parties came to prominence in the pre-1914 period – the Octobrists and the Kadets.

a) The Octobrists

This group dated from the issuing of the tsar's manifesto of October 1905, which established the duma. The Octobrists were moderates who were basically loyal to the tsar and his government. They believed in the maintenance of the Russian Empire and regarded the manifesto and the establishment of the duma as major constitutional advances. The Octobrists were mainly drawn from the larger commercial, industrial and landowning interests. Their leading members were Alexander Guchkov, a factory owner, and Mikhail Rodzianko, a large landowner, both of whom were later to play a leading part in the Provisional Government of 1917 (see page 85). How relatively limited the Octobrists were in their aims can be gauged from their programme, issued in November 1905, which called for:

1 unity amongst those who sincerely want the peaceful renewal of Russia and the triumph of law and order in the country, who reject both stagnation and revolution and who recognise the need for the establishment of a strong and authoritative regime, which, together with the
5 representatives of the people, could bring peace to the country through constructive legislative work.

The limited objectives of the Octobrists led to their being dismissed by revolutionaries as bourgeois reactionaries. This is far from accurate. In the dumas, the Octobrists frequently voiced serious criticisms of the short-sightedness or incompetence of the tsarist government.

b) The Constitutional Democrats (Kadets)

The Constitutional Democrats (known alternatively as the Party of the

People's Freedom) also came into being as a party at the time of the 1905 Revolution. The Kadets, the largest of the liberal parties, wanted Russia to develop as a constitutional monarchy, in which the powers of the tsar would be restricted by a democratically-elected constituent (national) assembly. They believed that such a representative body would be able to settle Russia's outstanding social, political and economic problems. Lenin dismissed this as bourgeois political naivety, but there is no doubt that the dream of a constituent assembly remained a source of excitement and inspiration to Russian reformers in the period before the 1917 Revolution.

The Kadet Programme
- an All-Russian Constituent Assembly
- full equality and civil rights for all citizens
- the ending of censorship
- the abolition of redemption payments on land
- the recognition of trade unions and the right to strike
- the introduction of universal, free education.

The Kadets were the party of the liberal *intelligentsia*, containing progressive landlords, the smaller industrial entrepreneurs, and members of the professions. Academics were prominent in the party, as typified by the Kadet leader, Paul Milyukov, who was a professor of history. The Kadets became the major opposition voice in the first duma and were instrumental in forming the Provisional Government following the February Revolution in 1917.

6 The 1905 Revolution

KEY ISSUES What grievances gave rise to the 1905 Revolution?
How revolutionary was the 1905 Revolution?
Did the 1905 Revolution leave the tsarist system weaker or stronger?

---

a) Background

The situation created by the government's policy of political repression after 1881 was graphically described by Leo Tolstoy (1828–1910), the great Russian novelist and social reformer:

i Russia lives under emergency legislation, and that means without any lawful guarantees. The armies of the secret police are continuously growing in numbers. The prisons and penal colonies are overcrowded with thousands of convicts and political prisoners, among whom the

5 industrial workers are now included. The censorship issues the most meaningless interdictions [bans]. At no previous time have the religious persecutions been so frequent and so cruel as they are today. In all the cities and industrial centres soldiers are employed and equipped with live ammunition to be sent out against the people. Yet this strenuous
10 and terrible activity of the government results only in the growing impoverishment of the rural population, of those 100 million souls on whom the power of Russia is founded, and who, in spite of ever increasing budgets, are faced with famine which has become a normal condition. A similar normal condition is the general dissatisfaction of all
15 classes with the government and their open hostility against it. Autocracy is a superannuated [hopelessly outdated] form of government that may suit the needs of a Central African tribe, but not those of the Russian people, who are increasingly assimilating the culture of the rest of the world. That is why it is impossible to maintain this form
20 of government except by violence.

(From Nicolai Tolstoy's 'Open address to Nicholas II', 1902)

The bleak picture that Tolstoy painted did not necessarily mean that confrontation, still less revolution, had to come. After all, if oppression is applied firmly enough it prevents effective challenges to government. What weakened the tsarist regime in the period before 1917 was not its tyranny but its incompetence. It is certainly true that the crisis which occurred in Russia in 1905 was in large measure due to the mishandling of the situation by the tsar and his government. This was to be shown by the speed with which the government reasserted its authority once it had recovered its nerve.

1905 marked the first time the tsarist government had been faced by a combination of the three main opposition classes in Russia – the industrial workers, the peasantry, and the reformist middle class. This was the broad-based revolt that most revolutionaries had been awaiting. Yet when it came it was accidental rather than planned. Despite the efforts of the various revolutionary parties to politicise events, the strikes and demonstrations in the pre-1905 period had been the result of economic rather than political factors. They had been a reaction to industrial recession and bad harvests. It was the tsarist regime's ill-judged policies that turned the disturbances of 1905 into a direct challenge to its own authority.

b) The Course of Events

The 1905 Revolution began with what has become known as Bloody Sunday. On 22 January, Father Gapon, an Orthodox priest and *Okhrana* double-agent, attempted to lead a peaceful march of workers and their families to the Winter Palace in St Petersburg. (The *Okhrana* were the state secret police whose special task was to hunt down subversives who challenged the tsarist regime.) The marchers' intention was to present a loyal petition to the tsar, begging him to use his royal authority to alleviate their desperate conditions. However, the march induced panic in the police authorities in the capital. The marchers were fired on and charged by cavalry. There are no precise figures of those killed, but the casualties seem to have amounted to hundreds. The killings were depicted by opponents of the tsarist regime as a deliberate massacre of unarmed petitioners. Although Nicholas II was in fact absent from St Petersburg when these events took place, they gravely damaged the traditional image of the tsar as the 'Little Father', the guardian of the Russian people.

The immediate reaction to Bloody Sunday was a nationwide outbreak of disorder, which increased as the year went on. Strikes occurred in all the major cities and towns. Terrorism against government officials and landlords, much of it organised by the SRs, spread to the countryside. The situation was made worse by Russia's humiliation in the war against Japan (see page 28). The government was blamed for Russia's defeat, which led to further outrages, including the assassination of Plehve by SR terrorists. One newspaper reported that:

> 1 Hundreds of buildings, worth several millions of roubles, have been
> destroyed. All the buildings have been razed to the ground on some
> enormous estates. Many houses have been burnt down without refer-
> ence to the relations which had existed between the peasants and the
> 5 landowners or the latter's political views.

An important factor in the dissatisfaction of the peasants was their fear that the government was about to seize the property of those families who had failed to pay off the mortgages taken out in the post-emancipation years (see page 24). The unrest and the government's difficulties in containing it encouraged the national minorities to assert themselves. Georgia declared itself an independent state. Witte remarked:

> 1 [Non-Russians], seeing this great upheaval, lifted their heads and
> decided that the time was ripe for the realisation of their dreams and
> desires. The Poles wanted autonomy, the Jews wanted equal rights, and
> so on. All of them longed for the destruction of the system of deliber-
> 5 ate oppression which embittered their lives. And on top of everything,
> the army was in an ugly mood.

In May, the Kadets, led by Milyukov, persuaded the majority of the liberal groups to join them in forming a 'Union of Unions', with the aim of organising a broad-based alliance that would include the peasants and the factory workers. A 'Union of Unions' declaration was issued:

> 1 All means are admissible in the face of the terrible menace contained in
> the very fact of the continued existence of the present government: and
> every means must be tried. We appeal to all groups, to all parties, all

organised unions, all private groups, and we say with all our strength,
5 with all the means at our disposal, you must hasten the removal of the
gang of robbers that is now in power, and put in its place a constituent
assembly.

The summer of 1905 brought the still more disturbing news for the
tsarist authorities of mutinies in the army and navy. In June, the crew
of the battleship *Prince Potemkin* murdered their officers and deserted
their squadron by sailing out of Russian waters. The end of the Russo-
Japanese War in August did little to ease the situation. Indeed, Witte
feared that the returning troops would join the revolution. If this happened, he said, 'then everything would collapse'. By the autumn, the
industrial unrest had grown into a general strike. It was in this atmosphere that a development of particular moment occurred. In a
number of cities, most notably in St Petersburg and Moscow, workers
formed themselves into an elected soviet (Russian for council). The
soviets began as organisations to represent the workers' demands for
better conditions, but their potential as bases for political agitation
was immediately recognised by revolutionaries. The Menshevik, Lev
Trotsky, became chairman of the St Petersburg soviet and organiser
of the general strike in the capital.

By October the tsar was faced by the most united opposition in
Romanov history. But at this critical juncture the regime began to
show the sense of purpose that it had so far lacked. Concession was
unavoidable, but by giving ground the government intended to divide
the opposition forces which confronted it. The liberals were the first
to be placated by the granting of a duma. On Witte's advice, the tsar
issued the October Manifesto in which he accepted the creation of a
legislative (law-making) duma. Since the manifesto also contained a
promise to introduce a range of civil rights, including freedom of
speech, assembly and worship, and the legalising of trade unions, the
liberals could claim a remarkable success. Their appetite for reform
was satisfied, at least temporarily.

The peasants were the next to be bought off by an announcement in
November that the mortgage repayments which had so troubled them
were to be progressively reduced and then abolished altogether. The
response was an immediate drop in the number of land-seizures by the
peasants and a decline in the general lawlessness in the countryside.

Having won over the liberals and peasants, the government was
now seriously opposed by only one major group – the industrial
workers. Here the policy was one not of concession but of suppression. The government felt strong enough to attempt to crush the soviets. Despite the mutinies earlier in the year, the troops who returned
from the Far East at the end of the war proved loyal enough to be
used against the strikers. After a five-day siege, the headquarters of
the St Petersburg soviet were stormed and the ringleaders, including
Trotsky, were arrested. The suppression of the Moscow soviet was

even more violent. Lenin, who had been slow to take advantage of the 1905 Revolution, arrived in Moscow in December, only in time to witness the flames of the gutted soviet buildings.

c) Significance

A notable feature of the 1905 Revolution was how minor a part was played by the revolutionaries. Hardly any of them were in St Petersburg or Moscow when it began. Revolution occurred in spite, rather than because, of them. With the exception of Trotsky, none of the SDs made an impact on the course of events. This throws doubt on the notion of 1905 as a revolution. There is the further fact that in a number of important respects tsardom emerged from the disturbances stronger rather than weaker. Despite its disastrous failure to win the war against Japan, which produced protest throughout Russia and united the classes in opposition, the tsarist regime survived 1905 remarkably unscathed. The mutinies in the armed services did not spread and did not continue after the war. Loyal troops returned to destroy the soviets. The readiness with which the liberals and the peasants accepted the government's political and economic bribes indicated that neither of those groups was genuinely ready for revolution. It is true that the tsar appeared to grant significant concessions in the October Manifesto, but these were expedients rather than real reforms. The duma was not intended to be, nor did it become, a limitation on the tsar's autocratic powers. This was evident from the Fundamental Laws, which Nicholas II promulgated in 1906:

> The Sovereign Emperor possesses the initiative in all legislative matters. The Fundamental Laws may be subject to revision in the State Council and the State Duma only on His initiative. The Sovereign Emperor ratifies the laws. No law can come into force without his approval.

The lesson of 1905 was that as long as the tsarist government kept its nerve and the army remained loyal, the forces of protest would find it very difficult to mount a serious challenge. The events of 1905 also raised questions about the extent to which the liberals wanted change in Russia. Few of them enjoyed their experience of mixing with the workers during the Revolution. They found proletarian coarseness unattractive and were frightened by the primitive forces they had helped to unleash. One middle-class proprietor, who had thrown his house open to the strikers, remarked on the difficulty of sustaining his belief in the goodness of people who abused his hospitality by molesting his daughters and spitting on his carpet. Peter Struve, who had been a Marxist before joining the Kadets in 1905, spoke for all frightened liberals when he said 'Thank God for the tsar, who has saved us from the people'.

Trotsky's later reflections on the character of the 1905 Revolution provides an apt summary of its essential characteristics:

ı   The events of 1905 were a prologue to the two revolutions of 1917.
    The Russo-Japanese War had made tsarism totter. Against the back-
    ground of a mass movement the liberal bourgeoisie had frightened the
    monarchy with its opposition. The workers had organised indepen-
5   dently of the bourgeoisie in soviets. Peasant uprisings to seize the land
    occurred throughout the country. Not only the peasants, but also the
    revolutionary parts of the army tended towards the soviets. However,
    all the revolutionary forces were then going into action for the first
    time, lacking experience and confidence. The liberals backed away from
10 the revolution exactly at the moment when it became clear that to
    shake tsardom would not be enough, it must be overthrown. This sharp
    break of the bourgeoisie with the people, in which the bourgeoisie
    carried with it considerable circles of the democratic intelligentsia,
    made it easier for the monarchy to differentiate within the army, sepa-
15 rating out the loyal units, and to make a bloody settlement with the
    workers and peasants. Although with a few broken ribs, tsarism came
    out of the experience of 1905 alive and strong enough.[2]

7 The Dumas 1906–14

> **KEY ISSUES** Were the dumas ever anything more than a talking
> shop?
> Did they represent an opportunity for tsarism to modernise itself?

There were four dumas in the years between the 1905 Revolution and
the February Revolution of 1917. The four elections produced the following results:

party or group	1st Duma 1906	2nd Duma 1907	3rd Duma 1907–12	4th Duma 1912–17
SDs (Mensheviks)	18	47	–	–
SDs (Bolsheviks)	–	–	19	15
SRs	–	37	–	–
Labourists *	136	104	13	10
Kadets	182	91	54	53
Octobrists	17	42	154	95
Progressists**	27	28	28	41
Rightists***	8	10	147	154
National parties	60	93	26	22
others	–	50	–	42
total	448	502	441	432

*The SRs as a party officially boycotted the elections to the first duma, but stood as
Labourists.
**The Progressists were a party of businessmen who favoured moderate reform.
***The Rightists were not a single party; they represented a range of conservative views
from right of centre to extreme reaction.

a) The First Duma, April–June 1906

The high hopes of the liberals that the granting of the duma marked a real constitutional advance were dimmed even before it first met. Having survived the challenge of 1905, the tsarist regime quickly recovered its confidence. Early in 1906, it successfully negotiated a substantial loan from France. This lessened the likelihood of the duma being able to exercise a financial hold over the government. A greater limitation on the duma's influence was the tsar's promulgation of the Fundamental Laws, which was timed to coincide with the opening of the duma. In addition to declaring that 'Supreme Autocratic Power' belonged to the tsar, the Laws announced that the duma would be composed of two chambers; one would be the elected duma, the other would be a state council, the majority of whose members would be appointed by the tsar. The existence of a second chamber with the power of veto deprived the elected duma of any genuine legislative control. Taken together with the declaration that no law could come into being without the tsar's approval, these restrictions made it clear that the tsarist regime had no intention of allowing the concessions it had made in 1905 to diminish its absolute authority.

The result was that the duma met in a mood of bitterness. The elections had returned a duma that was dominated by the liberal and reformist parties. They immediately voiced their anger at what they regarded as the government's reneging on its promises. They demanded that the rights and powers of the duma be increased. Goremykin, the chief minister, told them that their demands were 'inadmissible' and Nicholas II was reported as saying, 'Curse the duma. It is all Witte's doing'. After two months of acrimonious wrangling, the tsar ordered the duma to be dissolved. In frustration, 200 Kadet and Labourist deputies reassembled at Vyborg in Finland where they drew up an 'Appeal', urging the people of Russia to defy their government by non-payment of taxes and refusal to obey conscription orders.

The Vyborg Appeal was an ill-considered move. The response from the population was not national passive disobedience but scattered violence. This provided the government with a ready excuse for retaliation. The tsar appointed Stolypin as chief minister to act as his strong man. The Vyborg group were arrested and debarred from re-election to the duma. This was the prelude to Stolypin's introduction of a policy of fierce repression, which he sustained until his assassination in 1911. Martial law was proclaimed and a network of courts-martial, with wide-reaching powers, was used to quell disturbances. There were so many executions (over 2,500 between 1906 and 1911) that the hangman's noose became known throughout Russia as 'Stolypin's necktie'.

b) The Second Duma, February–June 1907

The Kadet failure in 1906 had important long-term effects. Although the Kadet Party survived under the leadership of Milyukov, it never really recovered from its humiliation. The liberal cause had discredited itself, thus allowing both the left and the right to argue from their different standpoints that the future of Russia lay either in socialist revolution or extreme reaction.

The immediate result was that in the elections for the second duma the number of Kadet seats was halved. The beneficiaries were the SDs and the SRs, who between them returned 188 deputies. Since the right also had greater numbers than in the previous assembly, there was considerable disagreement within the duma as well as between it and the government. Stolypin, who, despite his stern repression of social disorder, was willing to work with the duma in introducing necessary reforms, found his land programme strenuously opposed. The tsar was particularly incensed to learn of the duma's criticism of the government's administration of the army. Amid scenes of disorder, following government accusations that the SD and SR deputies were engaging in subversion, the second duma was dissolved after barely three months' existence.

c) The Third Duma, November 1907–June 1912

Despite the opposition shown by the first two dumas, the tsar made no attempt to dispense with the duma altogether. There were two main reasons for this. The first related to foreign policy. The tsar was keen to project an image of Russia as a democratic nation. He was advised by his foreign ministers, who at this time were in talks with France and Britain (see page 27), that Russia's new allies were considerably impressed by the existence of an apparently representative national assembly.

The second reason was that the duma had been rendered docile by the government's doctoring of the electoral system, so as to return an assembly from which the critics of tsardom were largely excluded. This had been achieved by Stolypin's introduction of new electoral laws which greatly restricted the right to vote. The new franchise laws effectively limited the vote to the propertied classes. In the election to the third duma, only one in six of the male population was entitled to vote. The peasants and industrial workers were virtually excluded. The consequence was (as the table on page 50 shows) that the third and fourth dumas were heavily dominated by the right-wing parties, a reversal of the position in the first and second dumas in which the radical parties had held a large majority.

With the balance of the parties redressed in this way, Stolypin developed better relations with the third duma, which enabled him to pursue his land reforms without opposition from the deputies.

This is not to say that the duma was entirely subservient. It exercised its right to question ministers and to discuss state finances. It also used its committee system to make important proposals for modernising the armed services. Among the 2,571 bills it approved were social reform measures that included a scheme of national insurance for industrial workers.

c) The Fourth Duma, November 1912–August 1914

It was Stolypin's tragedy, as it had been Witte's, that his abilities were never fully appreciated by the regime he tried to serve. Following his murder in 1911, the various ministers the tsar appointed were distinguished only by their incompetence. Since they lacked political imagination, their only course was further repression. Between 1911 and 1914 the regime's terror tactics were part cause, part effect, of a dramatic increase in public disorder, which gradually returned to the proportions of 1905. The number of strikes listed as 'political' by the Ministry of Trade and Industry rose from 24 in 1911 to 2,401 in 1914. The following extract from the report of a Moscow *Okhrana* agent in 1912 was typical of the news reaching the government:

> 1 There has never been so much tension. People can be heard speaking of the government in the sharpest and most unbridled tones. Many say that the 'shooting' of the Lena workers recalls the 'shooting' of the workers at the Winter Palace of January 9 1905. Influenced by ques-
> 5 tions in the duma and the speeches which they called forth there, public tension is increasing still more. It is a long time since even the extreme left has spoken in such a way, since there have been references in the duma to 'the necessity of calling a Constituent Assembly and overthrowing the present system by the united strength of the proletariat'.

The reference to the Lena workers recalled the notorious incident that occurred in 1912 in the Lena Goldfields in Siberia. Demands from the miners there for better pay and conditions were resisted by the employers, who appealed to the police to arrest the strikers' leaders as criminals. The issue thus became the much larger one of trade union rights in Russia. When the police moved into Lena the strikers closed ranks and the situation rapidly worsened, resulting in troops firing on and killing or injuring a large number of miners. The *Okhrana* appeared to have acted as *agents provocateurs* in order to identify the ringleaders of the strike.

The agent's report is also significant in its reference to the protests in the fourth duma, which although later described by post-1917 revolutionaries as having been a cowed, ineffectual, body was obviously capable of making spirited protest. The truth was that many moderates in the duma had begun to despair of the government's responding realistically to the problems that confronted Russia. Alexander Guchkov told the Octobrist Party conference in 1913:

1 [The] attempt made by the Russian public, as represented by our party, to effect a peaceful, painless transition from the old condemned system to a new order has failed. Let those in power make no mistake about the temper of the people; let them not take outward indications of
5 prosperity as a pretext for lulling themselves into security. Never were the Russian people so profoundly revolutionised by the actions of the government, for day by day faith in the government is steadily waning, and with it is waning faith in the possibility of a peaceful issue of the crisis.

In the following year the duma expressed its sense of impending catastrophe in a formal resolution:

1 The Ministry of the Interior systematically scorns public opinion and ignores the repeated wishes of the new legislature. The duma considers it pointless to express any new wishes in regard to internal policy. The Ministry's activities arouse dissatisfaction among the broad masses
5 who have hitherto been peaceful. Such a situation threatens Russia with untold dangers.

After 1917, it was usual for historians to follow the lead of Bolshevik critics in dismissing the later dumas as having been merely rubber stamps of government policy. However, modern scholars tend to be less critical. They refer to the dumas' frequent criticisms of government policy, their productive work in such areas as education and state insurance, and suggest that it was only the ineptitude of the tsarist government that prevented the dumas from making a greater contribution to the development of Russia.

8 Conclusion

> **KEY ISSUE** Was the period 1881–1914 a time of lost opportunity for tsardom?

The economic policies of Witte and Stolypin and the introduction of the duma were important advances, but they were not enough to alter the essentially reactionary character of the tsarist system. The government remained hostile towards reform. The industrial spurt of the 1890s had offered an opportunity for Russia to modernise herself, but a sustained policy of modernisation required not simply economic progress but a commitment to political change as well. This the tsar was never willing to give. His resistance to change would have mattered less if the system had operated efficiently. But the tsarist autocracy was both oppressive and inefficient, thereby alienating the progressive elements in society, which could see no possibility of real advance in Russia as long as government and administration remained in the hands of incompetents.

It was this that undermined the work of the few enlightened ministers, such as Witte and Stolypin, within the government. They were reformers but they were also loyalists. Indeed, it was their loyalty to the system that led them to consider reform as a way of lessening the opposition to it. The irony was that they were not trusted by the representatives of the very system they were trying to preserve. It is for this reason that historians have suggested that in failing to recognise the true worth of Witte and Stolypin, the tsarist regime unwittingly threw away its last chance of survival. By 1914, all the signs were that imperial Russia was heading towards a major confrontation between intransigent tsardom and the forces of change. It was to be the war of 1914–17 that would determine what form that conflict would take.

References

1   Leon Trotsky, *The History of the Russian Revolution* (Gollancz, 1985) p.239
2   Leon Trotsky, *The History of the Russian Revolution* (Gollancz, 1985) p.34

Working on Chapter 3

The groups who came to oppose tsardom during this period covered a wide political spectrum. One of your main aims in studying this chapter should be to gain an understanding of these shades of opinion. The Bolsheviks deserve close attention since they were ultimately to seize power and establish a regime that lasted for nearly three quarters of a century. You are likely to be asked a great deal about them. This is why you need to make sure that you have grasped the main features of Marxism, the theory on which both the SD parties based their politics. There is no need at this stage to go too deeply into the theory but be sure that you understand what is meant by the dialectic and the class war. Lenin is a crucial figure in this respect, and you should aim to familiarise yourself with his thinking. A grasp of the subsequent history of Russia down to 1924 and, indeed, beyond, requires a working knowledge of Lenin's concept of revolution.

Answering structured and essay questions on Chapter 3

Structured questions are the type that begin with such leads as 'Describe ...', 'Describe how ...', 'Show how ...', 'In what ways did ...?' and 'Describe the ways in which ...'. Typical questions based on the material in this chapter might be:

 1. Describe how the Populists aimed to bring about change in Russia.
 2. Describe the way in which SD Party split into Bolshevik and Menshevik factions in 1903.

Summary Diagram
Opposition to Tsardom 1881–1914

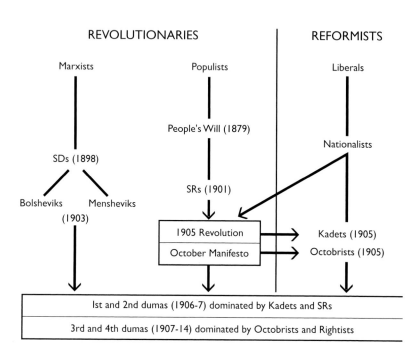

3. In what respects did the Bolsheviks and Mensheviks differ in their views on revolution?
4. In what ways did Lenin adjust Marxist ideas to make them fit the Russian context before 1914?'
5. Describe the difficulties encountered by the dumas between 1906 and 1914

The more difficult type of essay question either asks you to explain causation, that is to analyse why things occurred the way they did, or asks you to make a judgment on a historical proposition. The questions on causation are usually in a 'why?' form with such leads as, 'Why was …?', 'Explain why …' and 'Account for …'. Examples might be:

6. Why was the tsarist system faced with such a wide range of opposition in 1905?
7. Account for the inability of the revolutionary parties to gain from the 1905 Revolution.
8. Explain why the tsar was able to survive the 1905 Revolution with his power still intact.

Examples of questions calling for your judgment might be:

9. How far do you agree that the 1905 was a revolution without revolutionaries?

10. Examine the validity of the claim that the dumas between 1906 and 1914 were only a talking shop.

Consider question 8. The requirement is to explain why the tsar held on to his authority. Draw up a list of the opposition forces in 1905. Rank them according to their relative strength and importance. Then list the resources that the tsarist regime had at its disposal. Now ask yourself the question, 'Was the opposition powerful enough to be a real threat when set against the basic strength of the tsarist regime in 1905?' If you then pose yourself further supplementary questions you will find that an answer to the basic essay question will start to form. 'How significant was the coming together of the three social groups – liberals, peasants and industrial workers?' 'Was their union planned or merely accidental and superficial?' 'How soon did the regime recover its nerve?' 'Did not the events show that tsardom possessed sufficient political and military strength either to buy off or to smash the opposition?' It would be appropriate to refer to Trotsky's observations on 1905. He emphasised the inexperience and lack of confidence of the revolutionaries, stressed how the liberals had been frightened of revolution, and laid particular weight on the government's retention of the loyalty of the armed services. Since these ideas come from someone who was both an opponent of the regime and a prominent participant in the events of 1905, they merit a central place in your answer.

Source-based questions on Chapter 3

1. Lenin's Revolutionary Ideas
Study the extract from Lenin's writings on pages 40–1, and then answer the following questions:

a) What do you understand Lenin to mean by saying (line 2) that 'by its own ability the working class can attain only a trade-unionist self-consciousness'? (6 marks)

b) Using your own knowledge and the evidence in the extracts, examine Lenin's views on the role of the *intelligentsia* in revolution. (8 marks)

2. The 1905 Revolution
Read the extract from Tolstoy's address on pages 45–6 and from Trotsky's reflections on page 50. Then answer the following questions:

a) What features of tsarist repression does Tolstoy emphasise in this extract? (8 marks)

b) Using your own knowledge, assess the accuracy of Trotsky's explanation of the eventual withdrawal of the liberals from the 1905 Revolution. (10 marks)

c) How closely do the descriptions given by Tolstoy and Trotsky agree in their analyses of the forces opposing tsardom? (12 marks)

3. *The Dumas*

Study the table on page 50 and the extracts on pages 53–4, and then answer the following questions:

a) What does the table of election results reveal about the political shifts in the duma between 1906 and 1912? (6 marks)

b) According to the *Okhrana* agent's report on page 53, what part did the duma play in the creation of social tension in Russia? (8 marks)

c) To what extent do Guchkov's speech and the duma resolution on page 54 present different pictures of the political situation in Russia before 1914? (10 marks)

d) Assess the strengths and weaknesses of each of the three extracts as evidence for the role of the dumas between 1906 and 1914. (15 marks)

4 War and Revolution 1914–17

POINTS TO CONSIDER

This chapter considers three principal interlocking themes: the reasons why Russia went to war in 1914, the effect that the war had on the internal situation in Russia, and how this contributed to the downfall of tsardom in February 1917. Your aim during your first reading of the chapter should be to gain a clear picture of these developments. The narrative of the February Revolution is fairly detailed so you may need to read it a number of times.

KEY DATES

1914

28 June	Assassination of Franz Ferdinand at Sarajevo.
28 July	Austria-Hungary declared war on Serbia.
29 July	Russian full mobilisation orders given.
1 August	Germany declared war on Russia.
August	Suspension of fourth duma.

1915

June–July	The duma reconvened.
June	The Progressive Bloc formed in the duma.
August	Nicholas II made himself commander-in-chief of the Russian armies.

1916

November	Duma reconvened.
December	Rasputin murdered by a group of aristocrats.

1917

18 February –4 March	February Revolution
18 February	Strike began at Putilov factories in Petrograd.
23 February	International Women's Day saw the beginning of widespread workers' demonstrations.
25 February	A general strike began.
27 February	unofficial meeting of committee of duma coincided with the first meeting of the Petrograd Soviet.
28 February	Nicholas II prevented from returning to Petrograd.
1 March	Soviet 'Order Number 1' was issued.
2 March	Provisional Government formed from the duma committee. Nicholas II abdicated.

1 Russia's Entry into the First World War

KEY ISSUE Why was Russia drawn into war in 1914?

There were no clear signs that the tsarist government wanted war in 1914. Russia's experience ten years earlier against Japan had made it wary of putting itself at risk again, and its foreign policy after 1905 had been essentially defensive. It had joined France and Britain in the Triple Entente as a means of safeguarding itself against the alliance of the Central Powers, Germany and Austria-Hungary. However, the events that followed the assassination in June 1914 of Franz Ferdinand, the heir to the Austro-Hungarian throne, by Serbian nationalists made it virtually impossible for Russia to avoid being drawn into a European conflict.

By tradition, Russia was the protector of the Slav peoples of the Balkans. With the decline of Turkey, the old enemy, in the nineteenth century, Austria-Hungary was seen by Russia as the new threat. Sazonov, the tsar's foreign secretary in 1914, described the link between the commitment to defend Slav nationalism in the Balkans and Russia's long-standing strategic interests:

1   Russia's historical mission – the emancipation of the Christian peoples of the Balkan peninsula from the Turkish yoke – was almost fulfilled by the beginning of the twentieth century. Although these younger countries no longer needed the guardianship of Russia, they were not strong
5   enough to dispense with her help in the event of any attempt upon their national existence by warlike Teutonism [Germanic expansionism]. Serbia in particular was exposed to this danger, having become the object of the decorously concealed covetousness of Austrian diplomacy. Russia's sole and unchanging object was to see that those Balkan
10 peoples should not fall under the influence of powers hostile to her. The ultimate aim of Russian policy was to obtain free access to the Mediterranean, and to be in a position to defend her Black Sea coasts against the threat of the irruption of hostile naval forces through the Bosphorus.

A month after Franz Ferdinand's murder, Austria-Hungary, with German encouragement, declared war on Serbia. Russia still expected to be able to oblige the Austrians to withdraw, without itself having to go to war. It hoped that if it mobilised this would act as a deterrent to Austria. This was not unrealistic. Despite Russia's defeat by Japan, its armies were still regarded as formidable. Germans often spoke of 'the Russian steamroller', a reference to the immense reserves of manpower on which it was calculated that Russia could draw

It was at this stage that the great length of its western frontier became a critical consideration. Russia had two basic mobilisation schemes, partial and full. 'Partial' involved plans for a campaign in the south-west in defence of its Slav interests in the Balkans; 'full' involved plans for a general European war. Both forms of mobilisation were based on detailed railway timetabling aimed at transporting huge numbers of men and vast amounts of material. The complexity of the timetables meant that the adoption of one type of mobilisation ruled out the use of the other. The Russian fear in July 1914 was that if it mobilised only partially it would leave itself defenceless should Austria's ally, Germany, strike at Russia's East Prussian and Polish borders. On the other hand, full mobilisation might well appear to Germany as a deliberate provocation. The German government did, indeed, warn Sazonov that if Russia mobilised Germany would have to do the same. The fact was that, according to German contingency plans, if Russia mobilised war became unavoidable. The German 'Schlieffen Plan' was based on the concept of eliminating the danger to Germany of a two-front war against France and Russia by a lightning knock-out blow against France. Speed was of the essence. Germany could not play a game of diplomatic bluff; it had to strike first. The French ambassador in St Petersburg at the time described the fateful Russian decision:

> 29th July ... At eleven o'clock tonight, Basily [deputy director at the Russian Foreign Office] came to tell me that the imperious language used by the German Ambassador this afternoon has decided the Russian Government (1) to order this very night the mobilisation of the
> 5 13 corps earmarked for operations against Austria-Hungary, (2) secretly to commence general mobilisation.
>   These last words made me jump.
>   'Isn't it possible for them to confine themselves – provisionally at any rate – to a partial mobilisation?'
> 10   'No. The question has just been gone into thoroughly by a council of our highest military officers. They have come to the conclusion that in the existing circumstances the Russian Government has no choice between partial and general carried out only at the price of dislocating the entire machinery of general mobilisation. So if today we stopped at
> 15 mobilising the 13 corps destined for operations against Austria and tomorrow Germany decided to give her ally military support, we should be powerless to defend ourselves on the frontiers of Poland and East Prussia.'

The Russian full mobilisation order, eventually signed by an uncertain tsar on 30 July, had been intended as a diplomatic manoeuvre which would still leave Russia free to hold back from war. In the event, it was the step that precipitated war. On 31 July Germany demanded that the Russians cease their mobilisation. The following day, not having received a response, Germany declared war on Russia. Four days later Austria-Hungary did the same.

2 Russia at War

> **KEY ISSUE** To what extent did the 1914–18 War reveal the backwardness of the Russian state?

Nicholas had had reservations about war with Germany. In July he had exchanged a series of personal telegrams with his cousin, Kaiser William II, regretting the growing crisis in Russo-German relations. However, once war had been declared, the tsar became wholly committed to it. By 1917 the war would prove to be the undoing of tsardom, but in 1914 the outbreak of hostilities greatly enhanced the tsar's position. Nicholas became the symbol of the nation's resistance in its hour of need. Watching the great crowds cheering the tsar as he formally announced that Russia was at war, the French ambassador remarked: 'To those thousands the tsar really is the autocrat, the absolute master of their bodies and souls.' At a special session of the duma, all the deputies, save for the five Bolshevik representatives, fervently pledged themselves to the national struggle.

It was the same story in all the warring countries. The socialist parties abandoned their policies and committed themselves to the national war effort. Lenin was bitter in his condemnation of 'these class traitors'. He called on all true revolutionaries 'to transform the imperialist war everywhere into a civil war'. But the prevailing mood in Russia and Europe was all against him. The early stages of the war were dark days for Lenin's Bolsheviks. Vilified as traitors and German agents for their opposition to the war, they were forced to flee or go into hiding. Lenin, who was already in exile in Poland, made his way with Austrian help into neutral Switzerland. Had the war gone well for Russia there is good reason to think that the Bolshevik Party would have been hard pressed to survive.

But the war did not go well for Russia, and the reason was only partly military. The basic explanation for its decline and slide into revolution in 1917 was an economic one. Three years of total war were to prove too great a strain for the Russian economy to bear. War is a time when the character and structure of a society are put to the test in a particularly intense way. The longer the war lasts, the greater the test. During the years 1914–17, the political, social and economic institutions of Russia proved increasingly incapable of meeting the demands that war placed upon them. This does not prove that Russia was uniquely incompetent. The pressure of total war on all countries was immense and it should be remembered that of the six empires engaged in the First World War – Germany, Austria, Turkey, Russia, France and Britain – only the last two survived. Differing estimates have been made of Russia's potential for growth in 1914. But however that is assessed, the fact remains that the demands of the 1914–18 War eventually proved too heavy for Russia to sustain.

The impact of the war on Russia can be conveniently studied under four headings.

a) Inflation

Russia had achieved remarkable financial stability by 1914. 98 per cent of its bank notes were backed by gold and it had the largest gold reserves of any European country. This happy position was destroyed by the war. Between 1914 and 1917 over 1.5 billion roubles were spent on the war effort. The national budget multiplied from four million roubles in 1913 to 30 million in 1916. Increased taxation at home and heavy borrowing from abroad were only partially successful in supplying the capital Russia needed. The gold standard was abandoned, which allowed the government to put more notes into circulation. In the short-term this enabled wages to be paid and commerce to continue, but in the long-term it made money practically worthless. The result was severe inflation, which became particularly acute in 1916. In broad terms, between 1914 and 1916 average earnings doubled while the price of food and fuel quadrupled.

Prices (to a base unit of 100)		notes in circulation (to a base unit of 100)	
July 1914	100	July 1914	100
January 1915	130	January 1915	146
January 1916	141	January 1916	199
January 1917	398	January 1917	336

b) Food Supplies

To the growing problem of food prices were added the difficulties of food supplies. Military needs led to the requisitioning of farm horses and a drastic cut in the supply of chemical fertilisers. It was difficult to sustain agricultural output in such circumstances. However, the decline in food production should not be exaggerated. During the first two years of the war the grain yield was maintained at a slightly higher rate than the average for the five years before 1915. It was not until 1916 that it began to fall. Part of the reason was that inflation made trading unprofitable and so the peasants stopped marketing their produce and began hoarding their stocks. What increased the problems for the ordinary Russian in acquiring regular supplies was that the army had first claim on the more limited amount of food that was produced. The armed services also had prior use of the transport system. They commandeered the railways and the roads, with the result that food distribution to civilian areas became unreliable and inadequate.

Hunger bordering on famine was a constant reality for much of

Russia during the war years. Shortages were at their worst in the towns and cities. Petrograd (the Russian name for St Petersburg, adopted for patriotic reasons soon after the war began) suffered particularly badly because of its remoteness from the food-producing regions and because of the large number of refugees who swelled its population and increased the demand on its dwindling resources.

Daily civilian bread ration in Petrograd (in pounds weight)	
January 1916	2.7
December 1916	2.3
March 1917	1.8

c) Transport

It was the disruption of the transport system rather than the decline in food production that was the major cause of Russia's wartime privations. The growth of the railways, from 13,000 to 44,000 miles between 1881 and 1914, had been an impressive feature of Russia's economic development, but it still did not meet the demands of war. The integrated character of a railway network means that even a minor hold-up in one place can badly affect the whole system. The attempt to transport millions of troops and masses of supplies to the war fronts created unbearable pressures. Blocked lines and trains stranded by locomotive breakdown or lack of coal became increasingly common.

Less than two years after the war began, the Russian railway system had virtually collapsed. By 1916, 575 stations were no longer capable of handling freight. A graphic example of the confusion was provided by Archangel, the northern port through which the bulk of the allied supplies to Russia were sent. So great was the pile-up of undistributed goods that they sank into the ground beneath the weight of new supplies. Elsewhere there were frequent reports of food rotting in railway trucks that could not be moved. One of the tsar's wartime prime ministers later admitted: 'There were so many trucks blocking the lines that we had to tip some of them down the embankments to move the ones that arrived later.' By 1916 Petrograd and Moscow were receiving only a third of their food and fuel requirements. Before the war Moscow had received an average of 2,200 wagons of grain per month; by February 1917 this figure had dropped to below 700. The figures for Petrograd told a similar story; in February 1917 the capital received only 300 wagon-loads of grain instead of the 1,000 it needed.

d) The Army

A striking statistic of the Great War is that Russia, in proportion to its population, put fewer than half the troops into the field that either Germany or France did.

Numbers and percentages of the population mobilised

	1914	1918	total population	% of population mobilised
Russia	5.3 million	15.3 million	180 million	8.8
Germany	3.8 million	14.0 million	68 million	20.5
France	3.8 million	7.9 million	39 million	19.9
Britain	0.6 million	5.7 million	45 million	12.7

Yet in aggregate numbers the Russia army was still a mighty force. It had by far the largest army of all the countries that fought in the war. Its crippling weakness, which denied it the military advantage that its sheer size should have given it, was lack of equipment. This was not a matter of Russia's military underspending. Indeed, until 1914 Russia led Europe in the amount and the proportions it spent on defence.

The problem lay not in lack of resources but in poor administration and confused liaison. Despite commandeering the transport system, the military was as much a victim of the poor distribution of resources as the civilian population. In the first two years of the war the army managed to meet its supply needs, but from 1916 serious shortages began to occur. Rodzyanko, the president of the duma, who in 1916 undertook a special fact-finding study of conditions in the army, reported to the duma on the widespread disorganisation and its dismal effects:

> General Ruzsky complained to me of lack of ammunition and the poor equipment of the men. There was a great shortage of boots. The soldiers fought barefooted.

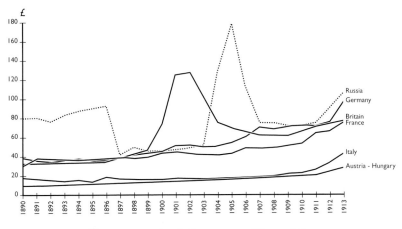

The comparative defence expenditure of the European powers, 1890–1913 (£million).

The hospitals and stations of the Red Cross, which came under my
5 notice, were in excellent condition; but the war hospitals were disor-
ganised. They were short of bandages and such things. The great evil
was, of course, the lack of co-operation between the two organisations.
At the front, one had to walk about ten or more versts from the war
hospitals to those of the Red Cross. [A verst is two thirds of a mile.]
10 The Grand Duke stated that he was obliged to stop fighting, temporarily for lack of ammunition and boots.
There was plenty of material and labour in Russia. But as it stood
then, one region had leather, another nails, another soles, and still
another cheap labour. The best thing to do would be to call a congress
15 of the heads of the zemstvos and ask for their co-operation.

The clear implication in Rodzyanko's account was that the strong
central leadership which the war effort desperately needed was not
being provided. This was a view that became increasingly widespread.
Nicholas had made the momentous decision in 1915 to assume direct
command of Russia's armed services. It was a gesture intended to rally
the nation around the tsar, but what it did was to make him personally responsible for Russia's performance in the war. If things went
badly he was to blame. Lack of success could no longer be blamed
upon his appointees.

The suffering that the food shortages and the dislocated transport
system brought to both troops and civilians might have been bearable
had the news from the war front been encouraging or had there been
inspired leadership from the top. But, despite occasional military successes, such as those achieved on the south-western front in 1916
when a Russian offensive under General Brusilov killed or wounded
half a million Austrian troops, took another 300,00 as prisoners, and
brought Austria-Hungary to the point of collapse, the gains made
were never enough to justify the appalling casualty lists. The enthusiasm and high morale of August 1914 had turned by 1916 into pes-
simism and defeatism. Ill-equipped and under-fed, the 'peasants in
uniform' who composed the Russian army began to desert in increasing numbers.

Care should be taken not to understate Russia's military capabili-
ties. Modern research, such as that undertaken by E.Mawdsley and
Norman Stone, has challenged the notion that the Russian army was
on the verge of collapse in 1917. Mutinies had occurred but these
were not exclusive to Russia. The strains of war in 1917 produced
mutinies in all the major armies, including the French and British.
Norman Stone dismisses the idea of a disintegrating Russian army as
a Bolshevik 'fabrication'. With all its problems the Russian armies
were still intact as a fighting force in 1917. Stone also emphasises the
vital role that Russia played as an ally of Britain and France in tying
down the Germans for over three years on the eastern front. An interesting detail, indicating how far Russia was from absolute collapse in

1916, is that in that year Russia managed to produce more shells than Germany. To quote these findings is not to deny the importance of Russia's military crises, but it is to recognise that historians have traditionally tended to exaggerate Russia's military weakness in 1917.

3 The Growth of Political Opposition to Tsardom

> **KEY ISSUE** Was the growth of opposition to the tsarist regime evidence of an 'institutional crisis' in Russia?

By 1916 all important sections of the population shared the view that the tsar was an inept political and military leader, incapable of providing the inspiration that the nation needed. It is significant that the first moves in the February Revolution in 1917, the event that led to the fall of tsardom, were not made by the political revolutionaries. The Revolution was set in motion by those elements of Russian society which in 1914 had been the most eager to rally to the tsar, but which, by the winter of 1916, were too wearied by his incompetence to wish to save him or the barren system he represented.

In August 1914, the duma showed its total support for the tsar by voting for its own suspension for the duration of the war. But within a year Russia's poor showing in the war led to its demanding its own recall. Nicholas II bowed before the pressure and allowed the duma to reassemble in August 1915. One major political mistake of the tsar and his ministers was their refusal to co-operate fully with the non-governmental organisations such as the Union of *Zemstva* and the Union of Town Councils, which at the beginning of the war had been wholly willing to work with the government in the national war effort. These elected bodies formed a joint organisation, *Zemgor,* which devoted itself to providing help for Russia's war wounded. The success of this organisation both highlighted the government's own failures and hinted that there might be a workable alternative to tsardom.

A similar political blindness characterised the tsar's dismissal of the duma's appeal to him to replace his palpably incompetent cabinet with 'a ministry of national confidence'. In rejecting this proposal, Nicholas destroyed the last opportunity he would have of retaining the support of the politically progressive parties. Milyukov, the Kadet leader, commented: 'They brushed aside the hand that was offered them. The conflict on the one hand between the representatives of the people and society on the other became an open breach.' Denied a direct voice in national policy, 236 of the 422 duma deputies formed themselves into a 'Progressive Bloc' composed of the Kadets, the Octobrists, the Nationalists and the Party of Progressive Industrialists.

The SRs did not formally join the Bloc but voted with it in all the duma divisions. Initially, the Bloc did not directly challenge the tsar's authority, but tried to persuade him to make concessions. However, as he and his government showed themselves increasingly incapable of running the war the Bloc became the focal point of political resistance.

The government continued to shuffle its ministers in the hope of

NICHOLAS II

-Profile-

1868   Born into the Romanov dynasty.

1894   Became tsar on the death of his father, Alexander III, married Princess Alexandra, the German grand-daughter of Queen Victoria.

1905   Granted the October constitution.

1906   Opened the first duma.

1913   Led the celebrations of 300 years of Romanov rule.

1914   Signed the general mobilisation order which led to Russia's entry into the First World War.

1915   Took over personal command of the Russian armed forces.

1917   Tried to return from HQ to Petrograd but prevented by rebellious soldiers and workers, advised by military high command and duma to stand down, abdicated on behalf of the Romanov dynasty.

1918   Nicholas and his family murdered in Ekaterinburg on Lenin's orders.

The character of Nicholas II is important in any analysis of revolutionary Russia. The evidence suggests that, though he was far from being as unintelligent as his detractors asserted, his limited imagination prevented him from fully grasping the nature of the events in which he was involved.

1   'His character is the source of all our misfortunes. His outstanding weakness is a lack of willpower.' (Sergei Witte)
    'The tsar can change his mind from one minute to the next; he's a sad man; he lacks guts.' (Rasputin)
5   'My poor Nicky's cross is heavy, all the more so as he has nobody on whom he can thoroughly rely.' (Empress Alexandra)
    'His mentality and his circumstances kept him wholly out of touch with his people. From his youth he had been trained to believe that his welfare and the welfare of Russia were one and the same thing,

10 so that "disloyal" workmen, peasants and students who were shot
down, executed or exiled seemed to him mere monsters who
must be destroyed for the sake of the country.' (Alexander
Kerensky).

15 'He has a naturally good brain. But he only grasps the significance
of a fact in isolation without its relationship to other facts.'
(Pobedonostsev)
'He kept saying that he did not know what would become of us all,
that he was wholly unfit to reign. He was wholly ignorant about
20 governmental matters. Nicky had been trained as a soldier. He
should have been taught statesmanship and he was not.' (Grand
Duchess Olga, his sister)

The tsar made a number of crucial errors in his handling of
the war, the most significant being his decision in 1915 to take
direct command of Russia's armed forces. This in effect tied the
fate of the Romanov dynasty to the success or otherwise of
Russia's armies. There are good grounds for arguing that the war
had offered tsardom its last great opportunity to identify itself
with the needs of modern Russia and so consolidate itself beyond
challenge as the legitimate ruling system. That opportunity was
squandered.

In 1914 there had been a very genuine enthusiasm for the
tsar as representative of the nation. Within three years that
enthusiasm had wholly evaporated, even among dedicated
tsarists. The fall of Nicholas was the result of weak leadership
rather than of savage oppression. He was not helped by his
wife's German nationality or by court scandals, of which
Rasputin's was the most notorious. But these were minor affairs
which by themselves would not have been sufficient to bring
down a dynasty.

finding a successful team. In the year 1915–16, there were four prime
ministers, three foreign secretaries, three ministers of defence, and
six interior ministers. It was all to no avail. None of them was up to the
task. The description by the British ambassador in Petrograd of one
of the premiers, Sturmer, might have been fairly applied to all the
tsar's wartime ministers:

1 Possessed of only a second-class mind, having no experience of
statesmanship, concerned exclusively with his own personal interests,
and distinguished by his capacity to flatter and his extreme ambition,
he owed his appointment to the fact that he was a friend of Rasputin
5 and enjoyed the support of the crowd of intriguers around the
empress.

The reference to Rasputin introduces the individual on whom much

Photo of one the many pornographic postcards that circulated in Petrograd in 1917. The word 'samoderzhavie' means 'holding'. It is used here as a pun to suggest Rasputin's hold on Russia as well as his physical holding of the Empress. Despite this cartoon and all the scurrilous things said about Rasputin and Alexandra then and since, it is highly unlikely they were ever lovers in a sexual sense. There is certainly no reliable evidence for it.

of the hatred of the tsarist system came to be focused. By any measure Rasputin's rise to prominence in Russia was an extraordinary story, but its true significance lay in the light it shed on the nature of tsarist government. Rasputin was a self-ordained holy man from the Russian steppes, who was notorious for his sexual excesses. As far back as 1907 he had inveigled himself into the imperial court on the strength of his reputation as a faith healer. The Empress Alexandra, desperate to cure her haemophiliac son, Alexei, the heir to the throne, fell under Rasputin's spell and made him her *confidant*. Scandal inevitably followed. Alexandra's German nationality had made her suspect and unpopular since the outbreak of war, but she had tried to ride out the storm. She would hear no ill of 'our dear friend', as she called Rasputin, and obliged her husband to maintain him at court. Since Nicholas was away at military headquarters for long periods after 1915, Alexandra and Rasputin effectively became the government of Russia. Even the staunchest supporters of tsardom found it difficult to defend a system which allowed a nation in the hour of its greatest trial to fall under the sway of a debauched monk. In December 1916, in an attempt to save the monarchy, a group of aristocratic conspirators murdered him.

From time to time there have been various attempts to present Rasputin in a more sympathetic light but any new evidence that appears seems to bear out the description given of him in the last paragraph. Where he does deserve credit is for his achievement in reorganising the army's medical supplies system. He showed the common sense and administrative skill that Russia so desperately needed and which his aristocratic superiors in government so lamentably lacked. It was his marked competence that infuriated those who wanted him out of the way. But no matter how much the reactionaries in the court and government might rejoice at the death of the upstart, the truth was that by the beginning of 1917 it was too late to save tsardom. Rasputin's extraordinary life as a courtier and his murder by courtiers were bizarre symptoms of the fatal disease affecting the tsarist system.

4 The February Revolution

> **KEY ISSUES** Were the events of February 1917 a collapse at the top or a revolution from below?
> Why was there so little effort to save tsardom in 1917?

a) The course of events

The rising of February 1917 was not the first open move against the tsar or his government. During the preceding year there had been a number of challenges. The Octobrists in the duma had demanded the removal of unwanted ministers and generals. What made February 1917 different was the range of the opposition to the government and the speed with which events turned from a protest into a revolution. Rumours of the likelihood of serious public disturbances breaking out in Petrograd had been widespread since the beginning of the year. An *Okhrana* report in January, 1917 noted:

1 There is a marked increase in hostile feelings among the peasants not only against the government but also against all other social groups. The proletariat of the capital is on the verge of despair. The mass of industrial workers are quite ready to let themselves go to the wildest
5 excesses of a hunger riot. The prohibition of all labour meetings, the closing of trade unions, the prosecution of men taking an active part in the sick benefit funds, the suspension of labour newspapers, and so on, make the labour masses, led by the more advanced and already revolutionary-minded elements, assume an openly hostile attitude towards
10 the Government and protest with all the means at their disposal against the continuation of the war.

On 14 February, Rodzyanko, the president of the duma, warned the tsar that 'very serious outbreaks of unrest' were imminent. He added ominously, 'there is not one honest man left in your entourage; all the decent people have either been dismissed or left'. It was this desertion by those closest to the tsar that unwittingly set in motion what proved to be a revolution.

The Revolution occupied the period from 18 February to 4 March 1917. (Down to February 1918, Russia used the Julian calendar which was thirteen days behind the Gregorian calendar in general use in most western countries.) A full-scale strike was started on 18 February by the employees at the Putilov steel works, the largest and most politically-active factory in Petrograd. During the next five days, the Putilov strikers were joined on the streets by growing numbers of workers, who had been angered by rumours of a further cut in bread supplies. It is now known that these were merely rumours and that there was still enough bread to meet the capital's basic needs. However, in times of acute crisis rumour often has the same power as fact.

23 February happened to be International Women's Day. This brought thousands of women onto the streets to join the protesters in demanding food and an end to the war. By 25 February, Petrograd was paralysed by a city-wide strike. Factories were occupied and attempts by the authorities to disperse the workers were hampered by the growing sympathy among the police for the demonstrators. There was a great deal of confusion and little clear direction at the top. Events which were later seen as having had major political significance took place in an atmosphere in which political protests were indistinguishable from the general outcry against food shortages and the privations of war.

The tsar, at his military headquarters at Mogilev, 400 miles from Petrograd, relied for news largely on the letters received from the tsarina, who was still in the capital. When he learned from her about the disturbances, Nicholas ordered the commander of the Petrograd garrison, General Khabalov, to restore order. Khabalov cabled back that, with the various contingents of the police and militia either fighting each other or joining the demonstrators, and his own garrison troops showing open insubordination, he doubted that the situation could be contained. Khabalov had earlier begged the government to declare martial law in Petrograd, which would have given him the power to use unlimited force against the demonstrators. But the breakdown of ordinary life in the capital meant that the martial law proclamation could not even be printed, let alone enforced. More serious still, by 26 February all but a few thousand of the original 150,000 Petrograd garrison troops had deserted. Desertions also seriously depleted a battalion of troops sent from the front under General Ivanov to reinforce the garrison.

Faced with this near-hopeless situation, Rodzyanko on behalf of the duma informed the tsar that only a major concession on the government's part offered any hope of preserving the imperial power. Nicholas, with that occasional stubbornness that he mistook for decisiveness, then ordered the duma to dissolve. It did so formally as an assembly, but a group of twelve members disobeyed the order and remained in session as a 'Provisional Committee'. This marked the first open constitutional defiance of the tsar. It was immediately followed by the boldest move so far, when Alexander Kerensky, a lawyer and a leading SR member in the duma, called for the tsar to stand down as head of state or be deposed.

On that same day, 27 February, another event took place that was to prove as significant as the formation of the Provisional Committee. This was the first meeting of the 'Petrograd Soviet of Soldiers', Sailors' and Workers' Deputies', which gathered in the Tauride Palace, the same building that housed the Provisional Committee. The moving force behind the setting up of the Soviet was the Mensheviks, who, had grown in strength in Petrograd during the war. These two self-appointed bodies – the Provisional Committee, representing the reformist elements of the old duma, and the Soviet, speaking for the striking workers and rebellious troops – became the *de facto* government of Russia. This was the beginning of what Lenin later called 'the dual authority', an uneasy alliance that was to last until October. On 28 February, the Soviet published the first edition of its newspaper *Izvestiya* (the News) in which it declared its determination 'to wipe out the old system completely' and to summon a constituent assembly, elected by universal suffrage.

The remaining ministers in the tsar's cabinet were not prepared to face the growing storm. They used the pretext of an electricity failure in their government offices to abandon their responsibilities and to slip out of the capital. Rodzyanko, who up to this point had struggled to remain loyal to the official government, then advised the tsar that his personal abdication was necessary if the Russian monarchy was to be saved. On 28 February, Nicholas decided to return to Petrograd, apparently in the belief that his personal presence would have a calming effect on the capital. However, the royal train was intercepted on its journey by mutinous troops who forced it to divert to Pskov, a depot 100 miles from Petrograd.

It was at Pskov that a group of generals from *stavka* (the army high command) together with representatives of the old duma met the tsar to inform him that the seriousness of the situation in Petrograd made his return both futile and dangerous. They, too, advised abdication. Nicholas tamely accepted the advice. His only concern was whether he should also renounce the throne on behalf of his son, Alexei. This he eventually decided to do. The decree of abdication that Nicholas signed on 2 March nominated his brother, the Grand Duke Michael, as the new tsar. However, Michael, unwilling to take up the poisoned chalice, refused the title on the pretext that it had not been offered to him by a Russian constituent assembly. Thus it was that the house of Romanov, which only four years earlier had celebrated its tricentenary as a divinely-appointed dynasty, came to an end not with a bang but a whimper.

By default the Provisional Committee, which had renamed itself the Provisional Government, thus found itself responsible for governing Russia. On the following day, 3 March, the new government officially informed the rest of the world of the revolution that had taken place.

b) the significance of the February Revolution

It is difficult to see the events of 18 February to 3 March as an overthrow of the Russian monarchy. What does stand out is the lack of direction and leadership at the top and the unwillingness at the moment of crisis of the tsarist generals and politicians to fight to save the system. Tsardom collapsed from within. Revolutionary pressure from outside had no direct effect. What is notable is that the Bolsheviks, absent from the 1905 Revolution, were also absent when the February Revolution took place. Practically all the Bolshevik leaders were in exile. Lenin, who was himself in Switzerland at the time, had not been in Russia for over a decade. With so many of the leading Bolsheviks out of the country for so long before 1917, and given the difficulties of communication created by the war, their knowledge of the situation in Petrograd in 1917 was second-hand and fragmentary. It is small wonder, therefore, that the events of February took them by surprise. Strong evidence of this is provided in a statement by Lenin to a group of students in Zurich in December 1916, only two months before the February Revolution. He told his audience of youthful Bolshevik sympathisers that although they might live to see the proletarian revolution, he, at the age of forty-six, did not expect to do so.

One remarkable feature of the Revolution was that it had been overwhelmingly the affair of one city, Petrograd. Another was the willingness of the rest of Russia to accept it. Trotsky observed:

> 1 It would be no exaggeration to say that Petrograd achieved the February Revolution. The rest of the country adhered to it. There was no struggle anywhere except in Petrograd. There was not to be found anywhere in the country any groups of the population, any parties, insti-
> 5 tutions, or military units which were ready to put up a fight for the old regime. Neither at the front nor at the rear was there a brigade or regiment prepared to do battle for Nicholas II.[1]

The February Revolution was not quite the bloodless affair that some of the liberal newspapers in Petrograd claimed. Modern estimates suggest that between 1,500 and 2,000 people were killed or wounded in the disturbances. But by the scale of the casualties regularly suffered by Russian armies in the war this figure was small, which further supported Trotsky's contention that the nation was unwilling to fight to save the old regime.

It should be re-emphasised that it was among tsardom's hitherto most committed supporters that the earliest rejection of the tsar occurred. It was the highest-ranking officers who first intimated to Nicholas that he should stand down. It was the aristocratic members of the duma who took the lead in refusing to disband on the tsar's orders. It was when the army and the police told Nicholas that they were unable to carry out his command to keep the populace in order that his position became finally hopeless. The strikes and demonstrations in Petrograd in February 1917 did not in themselves cause the Revolution. It was the defection of the tsar's previous supporters at the moment of crisis, compounded by Nicholas II's own failure to resist, that brought about the fall of the Romanov dynasty. Lenin once observed that a true revolution can occur only when certain preconditions exist; one essential is that the ruling power loses the will to survive. Some time before he formally abdicated, Nicholas had given up the fight. It was not the fact but the speed and completeness of the collapse of tsardom in February 1917 that was so remarkable.

What destroyed tsardom was the length of the war. A short war, even if unsuccessful, might have been bearable, as Russia's defeat by Japan twelve years earlier had shown. But the cumulative effect of a prolonged struggle proved overwhelming. Deaths and casualties by the million, soaring inflation, a dislocated communications system, hunger and deprivation, all presided over by a series of increasingly bewildered and ineffectual ministries under an incompetent tsar: these were the lot of the Russian people between 1914 and 1917. The consequence was a loss of morale and a sense of hopelessness that fatally undermined the once-potent myth of the tsar's God-given authority. By 1917 the tsarist system had forfeited its claim to the loyalty of the Russian people.

Many historians now interpret the February Revolution as the climax of an 'institutional crisis' in Russia. What they mean by this is that it was not economic difficulty or military failure that brought down tsardom. These were important but they were the symptoms rather than the cause. What produced the 1917 crisis in Russia was the failure of its institutions to cope with the problems it faced. Norman Stone writes:

> 1 Russia was not advanced enough to stand the strain of war, and the effort to do so plunged her economy into chaos. But economic backwardness did not alone make for revolution. The economic chaos came more from a contest between the old and the new in the Russian econ-
> 5 omy. There was a crisis, not of decline and relapse into subsistence, but rather of growth.[2]

Richard Pipes describes Russia in 1917 as:

> 1 a power that, however dazzling its external glitter, was internally weak and quite unable to cope effectively with the strains – political, economic, and psychological – which the war brought in its wake … the principal causes of the downfall in 1917 were political, and not econ-
> 5 omic or social.[3]

It is an axiom of modern history that a major war puts immense pressures on the nations involved. The war which Russia entered in 1914 had the effect of intensifying all the problems from which it had traditionally suffered. Russia's institutional crisis showed up the tsarist system as being politically as well as economically bankrupt.

References

1   Leon Trotsky, *The History of the Russian Revolution* (Gollancz, 1985) p.899
2   Norman Stone, *The Eastern Front, 1914–1917* (Penguin, 1998) p.304
3   Richard Pipes, *Three Whys of the Russian Revolution* (Pimlico,1998) p.30

Working on Chapter 4

Your aim in studying this chapter should be to gain an understanding of the causes of the February Revolution in 1917. The chapter was so shaped as to give the main sequence of developments from the outbreak of war in 1914 to the abdication of the tsar in 1917. You are recommended to follow this pattern when structuring your own understanding of the connection between war and revolution in Russia.

Summary Diagram
War and Revolution 1914–17

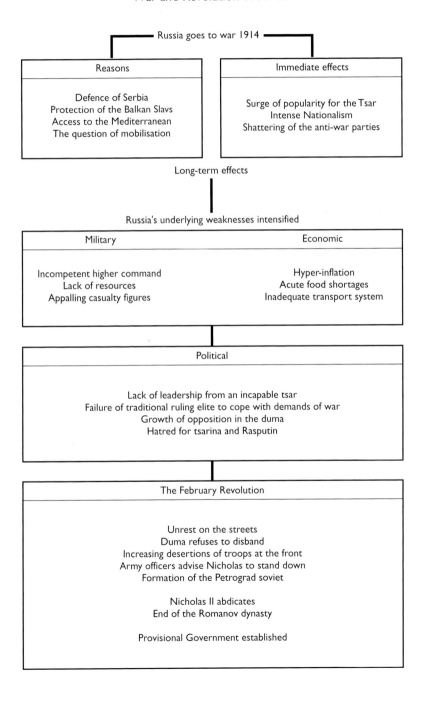

Russia goes to war 1914

Reasons	Immediate effects
Defence of Serbia Protection of the Balkan Slavs Access to the Mediterranean The question of mobilisation	Surge of popularity for the Tsar Intense Nationalism Shattering of the anti-war parties

Long-term effects

Russia's underlying weaknesses intensified

Military	Economic
Incompetent higher command Lack of resources Appalling casualty figures	Hyper-inflation Acute food shortages Inadequate transport system

Political

Lack of leadership from an incapable tsar
Failure of traditional ruling elite to cope with demands of war
Growth of opposition in the duma
Hatred for tsarina and Rasputin

The February Revolution

Unrest on the streets
Duma refuses to disband
Increasing desertions of troops at the front
Army officers advise Nicholas to stand down
Formation of the Petrograd soviet

Nicholas II abdicates
End of the Romanov dynasty

Provisional Government established

Answering structured and essay questions on Chapter 4

The following questions relate to each of the five main sections of this chapter.

1. a) Describe the stages by which Russia was drawn into war with Germany and Austria–Hungary in 1914.
   b) Explain the part played by the respective German and Russian mobilisation plans in bringing the two countries into war with each other in 1914.
2. a) Describe the difficulties faced by the Russian authorities after 1914 in trying to maintain adequate food supplies for the civilian population
   b) In what respects did Russia's war against Germany and Austria prepare the way for the February Revolution of 1917?
3. a) Examine the contribution of the duma to the Russian war effort between 1914 and 1917.
   b) How far do you agree that the Progressive Bloc represented 'the last hope of the tsarist system'?
4. a) Examine the view that the February Revolution of 1917 was 'not an overthrow from without, but a collapse from within'.
   b) Why was so little effort made to save tsardom in February 1917?'
5. a) Explain why Nicholas II's decision in 1915 to become commander-in-chief of the imperial army proved such a fateful one.
   b) How far was Nicholas II the author of his own misfortunes in1917?

Consider Question **4a**. Do not be deterred by the type of question that requires you to consider a challenging statement, such as the one quoted here. Indeed, rather than being discouraged, you should regard the quotation as a bonus, for what the examiners have done is to provide you with a very direct guide to the response they want from you. Think about how best to interpret the quotation. Be prepared to take time over this; it will be time well spent. In this instance, the quotation could be interpreted more simply as, 'Did tsardom fall or was it pushed?'. What you are being asked is whether Nicholas was toppled by anti-tsarist forces or whether it was his own weakness that obliged him to abdicate. From the notes you have made draw up two lists, one giving the opposition elements, the other containing the tsar's weaknesses. The main part of your answer should consist of these details arranged in such an order as to indicate which were of greater influence in bringing about the February Revolution. An important distinction to be drawn – and you are advised to devote a paragraph to this – is between the tsar's weakness as an individual and the weakness of tsardom as a system of government. It is reasonable to suppose that a stronger individual than Nicholas II as tsar might well have prevented the situation from deteriorating to the point of collapse. Another significant point to stress is that it was the traditional supporters of tsardom, the officer class and the duma, who began the open resistance to the tsar. It was their defection, not the crowds on the streets of Petrograd, that led Nicholas to regard things as hopeless.

Another point that examiners would expect you to make is that the debate on this issue has been considerably influenced by the wish of Bolshevik writers to present 1917 as a proletarian revolution made up of two phases, the first occurring in February. In their view, the overthrow of tsardom was part of the revolutionary process. You do not have to accept or reject this viewpoint, but let the examiner know that you are aware of it and balance it by saying that most disinterested historians emphasise that the absent Bolsheviks played no direct part in the events of February.

Source-based questions on Chapter 4

1. *Russia enters the war in 1914*
Study Sazonov's analysis on page 60, and the French ambassador's description on page 61. Answer the following questions:

a) According to Sazonov, what was the traditional aim of Russian foreign policy towards Turkey and the Balkans? (4 marks)
b) Using your own knowledge and the evidence in the French ambassador's account, explain why Russia's choice between full and partial mobilisation was so important in 1914. (5 marks)
c) From your own knowledge and your reading of these sources, how would you distinguish between the long-term and the immediate causes of Russia's entering the war in 1914? (6 marks)

2. *The Causes of the February Revolution*
Study Rodzyanko's report on page 66, the British ambassador's description on page 69, and the *Okhrana* agent's report on page 72. Answer the following questions:

a) In what ways does Rodzyanko's report reveal the disorganisation within the Russian army in 1916? (5 marks)
b) How appropriately might the account of Sturmer's character by the ambassador be applied as a general description of the quality of the tsar's wartime ministers? (10 marks)
c) How valuable to the historian are these sources as evidence of the tensions created by the tsarist government's handling of the war? (10 marks)

5 1917: The October Revolution

POINTS TO CONSIDER

The important point to stress about the Bolshevik Revolution in October 1917 is that it was quite distinct in character and objective from the revolution that had preceded it eight months earlier. The February Revolution had been essentially the collapse of tsardom from within. The October Revolution was a seizure of power by the Bolshevik Party from the Provisional Government, which had replaced the tsar but had proved no more capable of successfully leading Russia in wartime than he had. To understand how this second revolution came about it is necessary to chart the principal developments that occurred in Russia in the period from February to October 1917.

KEY DATES IN 1917

3 March	New Provisional Government publicly declared.
4 March	Formal declaration of Romanov abdication issued.
14 March	Petrograd Soviet issued its *Address to the people of the whole world*.
3 April	Lenin returned to Petrograd after completing his journey across Europe in a sealed train under German protection.
4 April	Lenin issued his *April Theses*, rejecting Bolshevik support for the Provisional Government.
26 June	Major Russian offensive launched against Austro-German armies on the south-western front.
3–6 July	Failure of 'July Days' Bolshevik uprising against the Provisional Government.
6 July	Lenin fled from Petrograd.
8 July	Kerensky became prime minister.
18 July	Kornilov became commander-in-chief.
August	German advance threatened Petrograd.
26 Aug –1 Sep	Resistance of the Petrograd workers forced Kornilov to abandon his march on the city.
25 Sep	Bolsheviks gained a majority in Petrograd Soviet and elected Trotsky as chairman.
7 Oct	Lenin slipped back into Petrograd.
10 Oct	Bolshevik Central Committee committed itself to armed insurrection.
12 Oct	Petrograd Soviet set up Military Revolutionary Committee.
23 Oct	Kerensky moved against the Bolsheviks by attempting to close down *Pravda* and *Izvestiya*.

Lenin instructed the Bolsheviks to begin the rising against Kerensky's government.
24 Oct First session of the Congress of Soviets.
24–25 Oct Bolsheviks took control of Petrograd.
25–26 Oct Kerensky fled from Petrograd.
Bolsheviks seized the Winter Palace.
26 Oct Bolsheviks established *Sovnarkom*, with Lenin as chairman.
27 Oct Lenin informed the Congress of Soviets that the Bolshevik-led Petrograd Soviet had taken power in their name.

1 The Dual Authority

> **KEY ISSUE** Was the Provisional Government fatally weakened from the first?

The Provisional Government, led by Prince Lvov, was the old duma in a new form. When Milyukov, the foreign minister, read out the list of ministers in the newly-formed government someone in the listening crowd called out, 'Who appointed you?' Milyukov replied, 'We were appointed by the Revolution itself.' In that exchange were expressed the two besetting weaknesses of the Provisional Government through-out the eight months of its existence. It was not an elected body. It had come into being as a rebellious committee of the old duma, refusing to disband at the tsar's order. As a consequence, it lacked legitimate auth-ority. It had no constitutional claim upon the loyalty of the Russian people and no natural fund of goodwill on which it could rely. It would be judged entirely on how well it dealt with the nation's problems.

The Provisional Government's second major weakness was that its authority was limited by its unofficial partnership with the Petrograd Soviet. It was not that the Soviet was initially hostile. Indeed, at first, there was a considerable degree of liaison between them. Some indi-viduals were members of both bodies. For example, Alexander Kerensky, the SR leader, was for a time chairman of the Soviet as well as a minister in the Provisional Government. The Soviet did not set out to be an alternative government. It regarded its role as supervi-sory, checking that the interests of the soldiers and workers were fully understood by the new government. However, in the uncertain times that followed the February Revolution, the Provisional Government often seemed unsure of its own authority. Such diffidence tended to give the Soviet greater prominence.

There was also the impressive fact that the soviet pattern had spread widely in the aftermath of the February Revolution. Soviets soon appeared in all the major cities and towns of Russia. The soviets were to play an increasingly important role in the development of the Revolution, but in the early stages they were not dominated by the

Bolsheviks and so were not necessarily opposed to the Provisional Government. It was significant, however, that even before the Bolshevik influence became predominant, the ability of the Petrograd Soviet to restrict the Provisional Government's authority had been clearly revealed. In one of its first moves as an organisation it had issued its 'Soviet Order Number 1':

> The orders of the military commission of the state duma are to be obeyed only in such instances when they do not contradict the orders and decrees of the soviet.

In effect, this Order, which was printed in *Pravda* and *Izvestiya* on 2 March, declared that the decrees of the Provisional Government in regard to military affairs were binding only if they were approved by the Petrograd Soviet. It is a commonplace of history that unless a government has control of its army it does not hold real power. What Order Number 1 made clear was that the Provisional Government did not have such power. It had, therefore, to compromise with the Soviet. Between February and April this worked as a reasonably effective consensus, which allowed a series of important changes to take place. A number of factors helped this 'dual authority' to operate. One was the euphoria experienced in Petrograd in the weeks following the collapse of tsardom. There was a genuine feeling across all the political groups that Russia had entered a period of real freedom. This made co-operation between potentially conflicting parties easier to achieve.

There was also a general acceptance that the new liberty should not be allowed to slip into anarchy and so destroy the gains of the Revolution. This created a willingness to maintain state authority at the centre of affairs. Furthermore, at the beginning both the Provisional Government and the Soviet contained a wider range of political representation than was the case later. Moderate socialists had a bigger influence than the SRs or SDs in the first meetings of the Soviet, while all parties, apart from the Bolsheviks and the monarchists, were represented in the Provisional Government during its early weeks. As the year wore on and the problems mounted, the Provisional Government moved increasingly to the right and the soviet increasingly to the left. But before that shift occurred there had been considerable co-operation.

The fruits of this were shown in such measures as an amnesty for political prisoners, the recognition of trade unions, the introduction of an eight-hour day for industrial workers, the replacement of the tsar's police forces with a 'people's militia', the granting of full civil and religious freedoms, and a commitment to the convening of a constituent assembly. However, the agreed changes did not touch on the critical issues of the war and the land. It would be these that would destroy the always tenuous partnership of the dual authority, and it would be Lenin who would begin the process of destruction.

2 Lenin's Return in April

> **KEY ISSUE** What impact did Lenin's return have on the situation in Petrograd?

Once the exiled Bolsheviks learned of Nicholas's abdication they rushed back to Petrograd. Those, like Stalin, who had been in Siberia were the first to return in March. Another group with Lenin at their head arrived from Switzerland in April. Lenin's return was a remarkable event. In the hope that the tsar's fall would be the prelude to the collapse of the Russian armies, the German government arranged for Lenin to return to Russia in a sealed train across occupied Europe. His German pass stated:

1 The carriage will be granted extra-territorial rights. No control or examination of passports or persons may be carried out either on entering or leaving Germany. Persons will be allowed to travel in the carriage absolutely regardless of their political opinions or their attitude
5 towards the question of the desirability of war or peace. As far as possible the journey shall be made without stops and in a through train. The *émigrés* may not be ordered to leave the carriage, nor may they do so on their own initiative. The journey may not be interrupted except in the case of technical necessity.

Lenin's wife, Krupskaya, recorded the event:

1 The moment the news of the February Revolution was received, Ilyich [Lenin] was all eagerness to get back to Russia. As there were no legal ways of travelling, illegal ways would have to be used. But what ways? From the moment the news of the Revolution was received, Ilyich had
5 no sleep. His nights were spent building the most improbable plans. Naturally the Germans gave us permission to travel through Germany in the belief that Revolution was a disaster to a country, and that by allowing emigrant internationalists to return to their country they were helping to spread the Revolution in Russia. The Bolsheviks, for their
10 part, considered it their duty to bring about a victorious proletarian revolution. They did not care what the German bourgeois government thought about it.

Since the outbreak of war in 1914 Lenin's opponents had continually accused him of being a German agent. Their charge had weight. Between 1914 and 1917 the German Foreign Office had given regular financial support to Lenin and the Bolsheviks, in the hope that if they achieved their revolutionary aims they would pull Russia out of the war (see page 106). As Krupskaya observed, Lenin did not really care what the attitude of the Germans was. It just so happened that, for quite different reasons, what they wanted – the withdrawal of the Russian armies from the war – was precisely what he wanted. However, it made no difference to anti-Bolsheviks that the German reasons were military and Lenin's were political. They considered the German government and the Bolshevik Party to be co-operating in a common cause, the defeat of Russia.

There is no doubting the great significance of Lenin's return to Petrograd in April 1917. Before then, the Bolsheviks had accepted the events of February, leading to the formation of the dual authority, as part of a genuine revolution. They had been willing to work with the other revolutionary and reformist parties. Lenin changed all that. In his speech on his arrival at Petrograd's Finland Station on 3 April, he declared that the February Revolution, far from giving Russia political freedom, had created a 'parliamentary-bourgeois republic'. He condemned the Provisional Government and called for its overthrow in a second revolution. The following day he issued his 'April Theses', in which he spelt out future Bolshevik policy.

Lenin insisted that the Bolsheviks abandon all compromise with other parties and work for the true revolution entirely by their own efforts. The role of the Bolsheviks was not to extend freedom to all classes, but to transfer power to the workers. This was a reaffirmation of his basic belief that only the Bolshevik Party represented the forces of proletarian revolution. Lenin had ulterior motives in demanding power for the soviets. Although he rejected much of what they had done, he saw the soviets as a power-base. In practice they had become an essential part of the structure of post-tsarist government. Lenin calculated that the soviets – the Petrograd Soviet in particular – offered his small Bolshevik Party the means by which it could obtain power in the name of the proletariat. The Bolshevik takeover of the soviets would be the prelude to Bolshevik takeover of the state.

Main points in Lenin's April theses

- February had not been a genuine class revolution but a palace *coup*, which had simply given authority to the bourgeoisie.
- The Soviet was the sole body with the right to govern.
- The Provisional Government was simply the old, class-ridden, duma in a new garb.
- It was the task of the Bolsheviks not to co-operate with the Provisional Government but to overthrow it.

The essence of Lenin's argument was summed up in a set of provocative Bolshevik slogans: 'Peace, Bread and Land' and 'All Power to the Soviets'. These proved to be more than slogans. They identified the basic problems confronting Russia: the war with Germany, the chronic food shortage, and the disruption in the countryside. It was the Provisional Government's failure to cope with these difficulties that was to bring about its collapse.

3 The Provisional Government

> **KEY ISSUES** Was the Provisional Government's problem not that
> it lacked power but that it did not use the power that it had?
> How were the Bolsheviks able to survive their failure in the July
> Days?

From the outset, the position of the Provisional Government was precarious. The dominant problem was the war. For the Provisional
Government after February 1917 there was no choice but to fight on.
Unless it did so it would no longer receive the supplies and war-cred-
its from the western allies on which it had come to rely. Tsardom had
left Russia virtually bankrupt. No government could have carried on
without large injections of capital from abroad. Foreign bankers were
among the first to visit Russia after Nicholas's abdication to ensure
that the new regime was committed to pursuing the war. The strain
that this obligation imposed on the Provisional Government finally
proved unsustainable. Its preoccupation with the war prevented it
from dealing with Russia's social and economic problems. It was a paradoxical situation: in order to survive the Provisional Government
had to keep Russia in the war, but in doing so it destroyed its own
chances of survival.

The question of the war brought about the first serious rift between
the Petrograd Soviet and the Provisional Government. On 14 March
the Soviet had issued an 'Address to the people of the whole world,
declaring for peace without annexations or indemnities'. Nonsense
was made of the government's acceptance of the 'Address' by the
repeated assurances of Milyukov, the foreign minister, that Russia
would continue to play its full military role as one of the allies. Late in
April, a series of violent demonstrations occurred in Petrograd
directed against Milyukov. These resulted in his resignation and that
of Guchkov, the war minister, early in May. In the reshuffled cabinet,
Kerensky become the war minister and places were found for leading
Mensheviks and SRs. It was hoped that this apparent leftward shift of
the Provisional Government would ease its relationship with the
Soviet.

In fact, the opposite happened. The socialists in the government
tended to become isolated from the Soviet. This was because in joining the government they had necessarily to enter into coalition with
the Kadets, which opened them to the charge that they were com-
promising with the bourgeoisie. Lenin wrote of 'those despicable
socialists who have sold out to the Government'.

Some individuals within the Provisional Government had misgiv-
ings about continuing the war, but at no time did the government as
a body contemplate withdrawing from the war. This would have mattered less had the Russian armies been successful, but the military

situation continued to deteriorate, eroding such support as the government had initially enjoyed. Lvov stayed as nominal head of the government but it was Kerensky who increasingly became the major influence. As war minister, he urged that Russia should embrace the conflict with Germany as a struggle to save the Revolution, requiring the total dedication of the nation. He made a number of personal visits to the front to deliver passionate speeches to the troops. He later described his efforts: 'For the sake of the nation's life it was necessary to restore the army's will to die. "Forward to the battle for freedom. I summon you not to a feast but death." These were the words I used before the troops in the front-line positions.'

This attempt to turn the war into a revolutionary crusade took no account of the real situation. The fact was that Russia had gone beyond the point where it could fight a successful war. Yet Kerensky persisted. In June, a major offensive was launched on the south-western front. It failed badly. With their already low morale further weakened by Bolshevik subversion, the Russian forces were no match for the Germans, who easily repulsed them and inflicted heavy losses. Whole regiments mutinied or deserted. General Kornilov, the commander on the south-western front, called on the Provisional Government to halt the offensive and direct its energies to crushing the political subversives at home. This appeal for a tougher policy was taken up by the government. Lvov stood down as prime minister, to be replaced by Kerensky. Kornilov became commander-in-chief.

The government's troubles were deepened by events on the island of Kronstadt, the naval base situated fifteen miles west of Petrograd in the Bay of Finland. Sailors and workers there defied the central authorities by setting up their own separate government. Such developments tempted a number of revolutionaries in Petrograd into thinking that the time and opportunity had come for them to bring down the Provisional Government. The attempt to do so became known as 'The July Days'.

a) The July Days

By the summer of 1917 it did, indeed, seem that the government's authority was irreparably breaking down. The spread of soviets, worker-control of the factories, widespread seizure of land by the peasants, and the creation of independent national minority governments – most notably in the Ukraine – suggested that the Provisional Government was no longer in control of events. It was the Ukrainian question that helped to provoke the July Days crisis. When the Kadet ministers in the coalition learned in late June that a Provisional Government deputation in Kiev had offered independence to the Ukraine, they resigned, protesting that only a constituent assembly could properly decide such matters. This ministerial crisis coincided with large-scale street demonstrations in Petrograd. Public protests were not uncommon; they had been almost a daily occurrence since February. But in the atmosphere created by the news of the failure of the south-western offensive and the government's mounting problems the demonstrations of early July turned into a direct challenge to the Provisional Government.

It is not entirely clear who initiated the rising of 3–6 July. A month before, at the first All-Russian Congress of Soviets, Lenin had declared that the Bolshevik Party was ready to take power, but the delegates had regarded this as rhetoric rather than a clear intention. It is also the case that there were SRs and other non-Bolshevik revolutionaries in the Soviet who for some time had been demanding that the Petrograd Soviet supersede the Provisional Government. Trotsky later referred to the July Days as a 'semi-insurrection' and argued that it had been begun by the Mensheviks and SRs. In saying this, he was trying to absolve the Bolsheviks from the blame of having started a rising that failed. The explanation offered afterwards by the Bolsheviks was that they had come heroically to the aid of the workers of Petrograd and their comrades-in-arms, the sailors of Kronstadt, who had risen spontaneously against the government. The opposite point of view was put at the time by Nikolei Chkheidze, the Menshevik chairman of the Soviet. He argued that the Bolsheviks, having been behind the rising from the beginning, later tried to disclaim responsibility.

The rising itself was a confused, disorderly affair. In the course of the three days the demonstrators fell out amongst themselves; those members of the Soviet who seemed reluctant to make a real bid for power were physical attacked. This disunity made it relatively easy for the Provisional Government to crush the rising. Troops loyal to the government were rushed from the front. They duly scattered the demonstrators and restored order.

While the origins of the July Days may have been uncertain, the results were not. The unsuccessful rising revealed a number of important facts: that the opposition forces were disunited, that the Bolsheviks were still far from being the dominant revolutionary party, and that the Provisional Government still had the strength to be able to put down an armed insurrection. This last revelation did much to raise the spirits of the Government and brought particular credit to Kerensky as war minister. Two days after the rising had been crushed he became prime minister. He immediately increased the pressure on the Bolsheviks. *Pravda* was closed down and many of the Bolshevik leaders, including Trotsky and Kamenev, were arrested. Lenin fled to Finland. Kerensky also launched a propaganda campaign in which Lenin and his party were branded as traitors and agents in the pay of the German high command. A fortnight after the July Days, the Bolshevik Party appeared to have been broken as a political force in Russia. What enabled the Bolsheviks to survive, as the next two

Photo of Lenin, clean-shaven and be-wigged, in hiding in Petrograd 1917.
Throughout the period April–October 1917, Lenin went in
constant fear of being arrested and executed by the Provisional Government.
He adopted various disguises, kept continually on the move and frequently
fled to Finland. Yet oddly, as Kerensky later regretfully admitted, the
authorities made little concerted effort to capture their chief opponent. This
raises the interesting question whether Lenin exaggerated, or the
Government underestimated, his powers of disruption (see page 97).

sections show, was the critical misjudgements by the Provisional Government over the land question and the Kornilov affair.

b) The Land Question

Land-shortage had been a chief cause of peasant unrest since the emancipation of the serfs in 1861. The February Revolution had led the peasants to believe that they would be the beneficiaries of a major land redistribution. They had expected that the estates of the land-lords would be appropriated and given to them. When this did not happen, the peasants in many parts of Russia took the law into their own hands and seized the property of local landlords. Disturbances in the countryside occurred daily throughout 1917. It would not be an exaggeration to describe this as a national peasants' revolt.

Neither the Provisional Government nor the Bolsheviks had a real answer to the land problem. The Provisional Government had set up a Land Commission with the object of redistributing land, but this body made little headway in handling a massive administrative task. It was doubtful, moreover, whether the Government's heart was ever really in land reform. The majority of its members came from the propertied classes. They were unlikely to be enthusiasts for a policy that would threaten their own position. They had supported the February Revolution as a political change, not as a social upheaval. They were quite willing for the estates of the fallen monarchy go to the peasants, but they had no intention of losing their own posses-sions in a general land redistribution. This had been the thrust of Lenin's assertion in the 'April Theses' that tsardom had been replaced not by a revolutionary but by a bourgeois regime.

Yet there was a sense in which the land issue was equally difficult for the Bolsheviks. As a Marxist party, they had dismissed the peas-antry as, in Trotsky's words, 'the pack animal' of history, lacking true revolutionary initiative. By definition the proletarian revolution was an affair of the industrial working class. Lenin, on his return in April, had declared: 'It is not possible for a proletarian party to rest its hopes at this time on a community of interest with the peasantry'. However, faced with the fact of peasant land-seizures throughout Russia, Lenin was quite prepared to make a tactical adjustment. Appreciating that it was impossible to ignore the disruptive behaviour of four-fifths of the population, he asserted that the special circumstances of post-tsarist Russia had produced a situation in which the peasants were acting as a truly revolutionary force. This modification of Marxist theory thus allowed Lenin to add the Russian peasants to the proletarian cause.

'Land to the Peasants', a slogan lifted from the programme of the SRs, became the new Bolshevik catchphrase. What this meant in mid-1917 was that the Bolsheviks recognised the peasant land-seizures as a *fait accompli*. Lenin declared that what the peasantry had done was wholly in keeping with 'revolutionary legality'. This produced a considerable swing to the Bolsheviks in the countryside. It had the further effect of splitting the SRs, a significant number of whom began to align themselves with the Bolsheviks. Known as Left SRs, they sided with the Bolshevik Party on all major issues.

c) The Kornilov Affair

In August, the Provisional Government became involved in the Kornilov Affair, a crisis that undermined the gains it had made from its handling of the July Days and allowed the Bolsheviks to recover from their humiliation. Parts of the story have been obscured by the conflicting descriptions later given by some of the participants, but there was little doubt as to the intentions of the chief figure in the episode. General Kornilov, the new commander-in-chief, was the type of right-wing army officer who had never accepted the February Revolution. He believed that before Russia could fulfil its patriotic duty of defeating Germany, it must first destroy the socialist enemies within. 'It's time to hang the German supporters and spies, with Lenin at their head, and to disperse the Soviet.'

By late August, the advance of German forces deeper into Russia began to threaten Petrograd itself. Large numbers of refugees and deserters flocked into the city, heightening the tension there and creating serious disorder. Kornilov declared that Russia was about to topple into anarchy and that the government stood in grave danger of a socialist-inspired insurrection. He informed Kerensky that he intended to bring his loyal troops to Petrograd to save the Provisional Government from being overthrown.

Accounts tend to diverge at this point in their description of Kerensky's response. Those who believe that he was involved in a plot with Kornilov to destroy the Soviet and set up a dictatorship argue that Kerensky had at first fully supported this move, and that it was only subsequently, when he realised that Kornilov was also intent on removing the Provisional Government and establishing military rule, that he turned against him. Other commentators, sympathetic to Kerensky, maintain that he had not colluded with Kornilov and that his actions had been wholly consistent. They also point to the fact that a special Commission of Enquiry into the affair in 1917 cleared Kerensky of any complicity. But however the question of collusion is decided, it was certainly the case that Kerensky publicly condemned Kornilov's advance. He ordered him to surrender his post and placed Petrograd under martial law. Kornilov reacted by sending an open telegram, declaring:

1 People of Russia! Our great motherland is dying. I, General Kornilov declare that under pressure of the Bolshevik majority in the soviets, the Provisional Government is acting in complete accord with the plans of the German General Staff. It is destroying the army and is undermining
5 the very foundations of the country.

In response Kerensky called on all loyal citizens to take up arms to defend the city. The Bolsheviks were released from prison or came out of hiding to collect the weapons issued by the Provisional Government to all who were willing to fight. By this strange twist in the story of 1917, the Bolsheviks found themselves being given arms by the very government they were pledged to overthrow. As it happened, the weapons were not needed against Kornilov. The railway workers refused to operate the trains to bring his army to Petrograd. When he received the news of this and of a mass workers' militia formed to oppose him, Kornilov abandoned the advance and allowed himself to be arrested.

It was the Bolsheviks who gained most from the failure of Kornilov's attempted *coup*. They had been able to present themselves as defenders of Petrograd and the Revolution, thus wiping out the memories of the debacle of the July Days. Despite the obvious readiness of the people of Petrograd to resist a military takeover, the Kornilov episode did not strengthen the position of the Provisional Government. Kerensky later admitted that the affair had been 'the prelude to the October Revolution'. It had further exposed the political weakness of the Government and had shown how vulnerable it was to military threat.

4 The October Revolution

> **KEY ISSUES** How vital was Lenin to the success of the Bolshevik rising?
> Were the Bolsheviks pushing against an open door in October 1917?

The measure of the Bolsheviks' recovery was soon apparent. By the middle of September they had gained a majority in both the Petrograd and Moscow Soviets. However, this should not be seen as indicating a large swing of opinion in their favour, but rather as a reflection of the changing character of the soviets. In the first few months after the February Revolution the meetings of the soviets had been fully attended. Over 3,000 deputies had packed into the gatherings of the Petrograd Soviet at the Tauride Palace. But as the months passed, enthusiasm waned. By the autumn of 1917 attendance was often down to a few hundred. This was a major advantage to the Bolsheviks. Their political dedication meant that they continued to turn up in force while the members of the other parties attended irregularly. The result was that the Bolshevik Party exerted an influence out of proportion to its numbers. This was especially the case in regard to the composition of the various sub-committees.

Broadly what happened in Petrograd following the Kornilov Affair was that the Petrograd Soviet moved to the left while the Provisional Government shifted to the right. This made some form of clash between the two bodies increasingly likely. Lenin put it as a matter of stark choice: 'Either a soviet government or Kornilovism. There is no middle course.' From his exile in Finland, Lenin constantly urged his party to prepare for the immediate overthrow of Kerensky's government. He claimed that his earlier estimate of what would happen had proved wholly correct: that the Provisional Government, incapable of solving the war and land questions, would become increasingly reactionary while the soviet would become the only hope of true revolutionaries. He further argued that the Bolsheviks could not wait; they must seize the moment while the government was at its most vulnerable. In a sentence that was to become part of Bolshevik folklore, Lenin wrote on 12 September: 'History will not forgive us if we do not assume power'.

Lenin's urgency arose from his anxiety in regard to two events that were due to take place in the autumn, and which he calculated would seriously limit the Bolsheviks' future freedom of action. One was the meeting of the All-Russian Congress of Soviets in late October; the other was the November election for the Constituent Assembly. He was convinced that the Bolsheviks would have to take power before these events occurred. If the Bolsheviks, under the banner 'All Power to the Soviets', could topple the Provisional Government before the congress met they could then present their new authority as a *fait accompli* which the Congress would have no reason to reject. The elections to the Constituent Assembly presented a different problem. The Assembly was the body on which all progressives and reformers had set their hopes. Once it came into being its moral authority would be difficult to challenge. Lenin told his party that since it was impossible to foretell how successfully they would perform in the elections, they would have to be in power before the results were announced. This would provide the Bolsheviks with the authority to undermine the results should they prove unfavourable.

At the same time as Lenin pressed this policy upon his party, Kerensky tried to make his government less exposed by announcing plans for a 'Pre-Parliament', a body intended to fill the interim before the Constituent Assembly came into being. Lenin condemned the Pre-Parliament as a manoeuvre to strengthen the bourgeoisie's grip on the government. Acting on his orders, the Bolshevik members of the Soviet who were entitled to attend the Pre-Parliament first derided it and then walked out.

Despite the power with which Lenin put his arguments to his colleagues, there were Bolsheviks on the Central Committee of the party who doubted the wisdom of striking against the Provisional Government at this point. In an effort to enforce conformity, Lenin slipped back into Petrograd on 7 October. His personal presence stiffened Bolshevik resolve, but did not produce total unity. During the next two weeks he spent exhausting hours at a series of Central Committee meetings trying to convince the waverers. On 10 October, the Central Committee pledged itself to an armed insurrection, but failed to agree on a specific date. In the end, by another quirk of fate, it was Kerensky and the government, not the Bolsheviks, who initiated the actual rising.

Rumours of an imminent Bolshevik *coup* had been circulating for some weeks, but it was not until an article, written by two members of the Bolshevik Central Committee, appeared in a revolutionary journal that the authorities felt they had sure proof. The writers, Zinoviev and Kamenev, argued that it would be a mistake to attempt to overthrow the government in current circumstances. Kerensky interpreted the article as indicating that a date had been set. Rather than wait to be caught off guard, he ordered a pre-emptive attack on the Bolsheviks. On 23 October, the Bolshevik newspapers, *Pravda* and *Izvestiya*, were closed down by government troops and an attempted round-up of the leading Bolsheviks began. The Bolsheviks no longer had a choice; Lenin ordered the planned insurrection to begin.

That there was a plan at all was the work not of Lenin but of Trotsky. While it was Lenin who was undoubtedly the great influence behind the October Rising, it was Trotsky who actually organised it. The key to Trotsky's success in this was his chairmanship of the Petrograd Soviet, to which he had been elected in September. As the dominant member of the three-man Military Revolutionary Committee (MRC) of the Soviet, it was Trotsky who had drafted the plans for the overthrow of the Provisional Government. When Lenin gave the order for the uprising to begin, it was Trotsky who directed the Red Guards in their seizure of the key installations and vantage points in Petrograd.

In the three days (25–27 October) that it took for the city to fall under Bolshevik control there was remarkably little fighting. There appears to have been no more than five fatalities during the whole episode. The simple fact was that the Provisional Government had hardly any military resources on which to call. Desertions had reduced the Petrograd garrison to a few loyal officer-cadets, a small group of Cossacks, and a battalion of women soldiers, known as the 'Amazons'. Faced by the Red Guards, the Cossacks deserted, while the cadets and the Amazons were persuaded that attempts to resist would be futile. When the Red Guards approached the Winter Palace, which housed the Provisional Government, they met minimal resistance. The sounding of its guns by the cruiser *Aurora*, moored in the River Neva, whose crew had declared their support for the Soviet, convinced the remaining members of the government that their position was hopeless. As many as were able escaped unnoticed out of the building. Kerensky himself, having earlier left the city in a vain effort to raise loyal troops, fled to the American embassy and subsequently to the USA.

A contingent of Amazons being trained in 1917. Kerensky had specially recruited these female soldiers as an example of the fighting spirit of the Russian people.

On the night of 27 October, Lenin informed the somewhat bewildered delegates to the Congress of Soviets, who had begun their first session that evening, that the Bolshevik-led Petrograd Soviet had seized power in their name. He then proceeded to read out the list of commissars (ministers) of the new revolutionary government (*Sovnarkom*). His own name was at the head as chairman. The right-wing SRs and the Mensheviks walked out, protesting that it had been a Bolshevik *coup*, not a soviet assumption of power. Trotsky jeered after them that they and their kind had 'consigned themselves to the dustbin of history'. Lenin then announced to the Bolsheviks and the SRs who remained that they would now proceed 'to construct the towering edifice of socialist society'.

The failure of the Provisional Government to rally effective military support in its hour of need was symptomatic of its much deeper political failure over the previous eight months. It was not that the Provisional Government was bitterly rejected by the Russian people. It was more a matter of its inability to arouse genuine enthusiasm. Kerensky's government had come nowhere near to solving Russia's problems or satisfying its needs. Its support had evaporated. Economically incompetent and militarily disastrous, the Provisional Government was not considered worth struggling to save. In October 1917, the Bolsheviks were pushing against an already open door.

5 Reasons for Bolshevik Success

> **KEY ISSUE** Why was it the Bolsheviks, and not any of the other parties, who took power in October 1917?

Trotsky later ascribed the success of the Bolshevik rising to three factors: 'the refusal of the Petrograd garrison to side with the government, the creation of the MRC, and the infiltration by Bolshevik commissars of the key divisions of the army'. These, he wrote, 'completely isolated not only the general staff of the Petrograd zone, but also the government'.

An obvious question is why none of the other parties was able to mount a serious challenge to the Bolsheviks for the leadership of the Revolution between February and October. One answer is that they had all accepted February as a genuine revolution. Consequently it made sense for them to co-operate with the Provisional Government, which claimed to represent the progressive forces in Russia. The result was that the supposedly revolutionary parties were prepared to enter into coalition with the Kadets, the dominant party in the government, and await the convening of the Constituent Assembly. This gave the Bolsheviks a powerful propaganda weapon, which Lenin exploited. He charged the socialists with having sold out to the bourgeoisie.

Another explanation is that the other parties were weakened by their support for the war. None of them opposed the continuation of the struggle against Germany with the consistency that Lenin's Bolsheviks did after April 1917. The non-Bolshevik parties regarded it as Russia's duty to defeat the enemy. The SRs, the Mensheviks and, indeed, some Bolsheviks believed wholeheartedly in a revolutionary war against bourgeois Germany. On the left of the Menshevik Party there was a vociferous wing of international revolutionaries who saw the war as the ideal opportunity for beginning the worldwide class struggle.

As committed Marxists, the Mensheviks had good reason for co-operating with the Provisional Government rather than opposing it. They saw the February Revolution as marking a critical stage in the class war, when the bourgeoisie had overthrown the old feudal forces represented by the tsar. This stage, as Marx had argued, was the necessary prelude to the revolution of the proletariat. However, the Mensheviks judged that since Russia did not yet possess a proletariat large enough to be a truly revolutionary force, it was their immediate task to align themselves with the other parties in a broad front to work for the consolidation of the bourgeois revolution before turning to the ultimate objective of the proletarian rising. One of the interesting paradoxes of the Russian Revolution is that, in strictly theoretical terms, the Mensheviks were always more consistent in their Marxism than were Lenin and his Bolsheviks.

In this context it is important to remember the lack of a tradition of legitimate party politics in tsarist Russia. With the fall of tsardom, the various parties found themselves for a brief, heady period free to advance their views. But there were no accepted rules of political conduct which they could follow. The arts of negotiation and compromise, which had developed in more advanced political systems elsewhere, were unknown in Russia. In their absence, politics was reduced to a simple question of who could gain power and then assert it over others. Lenin expressed it in the simple formulation: 'who, whom?' Democracy did not enter into it. Power would go to the most flexible and the most ruthless party. The Bolsheviks under Lenin perfectly fitted this requirement. They were prepared to adjust to circumstance if the occasion demanded. Their land policy was evidence of this. But they never lost sight of their basic goal – the seizure of power.

This did not make their position unassailable; the near-fiasco of the July Days had shown how narrow the gap between success and failure could be. Nor can it be said that their takeover in October was inevitable – that depended as much on the weakness and mistakes of their opponents as upon their own resolution. Yet what is clear is that none of the contending parties was as well equipped as the Bolsheviks to exploit the crises facing Russia in 1917.

Tseretelli, a Menshevik and a leading member of the Petrograd Soviet before its domination by the Bolsheviks, admitted: 'Everything we did at that time was a vain effort to hold back a destructive elemental flood with a handful of insignificant chips'. Struve, a liberal *émigré*, observed: 'Only Bolshevism was logical about revolution and true to its essence, and therefore in the revolution it conquered'. Milyukov, the Kadet leader, shared Struve's view of the Bolsheviks: 'They knew where they were going, and they went in the direction which they had chosen once and for all toward a goal which came nearer with every new, unsuccessful, experiment of compromise'.

Lenin's Bolsheviks were a new breed of politician: utterly self-confident, scornful of all other parties and ideas, and totally loyal to their leader. As Trotsky expressed it: 'The party in the last analysis is always right, because the party is the only historical instrument given to the proletariat to resolve its fundamental tasks'. Their ruthlessness did not guarantee their success, but it did mean that no other party could hope to gain or hold power unless it was able to overcome the challenge of these dedicated revolutionaries. In the event, none of the other parties was ever in a position to do this.

In assessing the reasons why the Provisional Government did not survive, it should be emphasised that it had never been meant to last. As its very title suggested, it was intended to be an interim government. Along with its partner in the dual authority, the Petrograd Soviet, its role was to provide a caretaker administration until an all-Russian Constituent Assembly was formed after the autumn election. The Assembly was the ultimate dream of all liberals and democrats; it would be the first fully-elected, nationwide, democratic parliament in Russia. All parties, including the Bolsheviks, were committed to it. As a consequence, the Provisional Government was always open to the charge that as an unelected, self-appointed body it had no right to exercise the authority that properly belonged to the Constituent Assembly alone. Such limited strength as the Provisional Government had came from its claim to be the representative of the February Revolution. Lenin had made it his task to undermine that claim.

One of the ironies of the situation was that both the Provisional Government and the Bolsheviks overestimated each other's strength, each delaying their moves against the other for fear of overplaying their hand. Historians have often wondered why the Provisional Government did not make a more sustained effort to destroy the Bolsheviks politically. It is true that some arrests were made, but the government's efforts at suppression were half-hearted and desultory. Sukhanov, a Menshevik eye-witness of the events of 1917, calculated that so limited was the Bolshevik military strength at the time of the October Rising that 'a good detachment of 500 men would have been enough to liquidate Smolny [the Bolshevik headquarters] and everybody in it'. Trotsky agreed, but asked derisively where the Provisional Government was to get five hundred good men to support it.

For their part, the Bolsheviks miscalculated the strength and effectiveness of the Provisional Government. Lenin expected to be summarily shot if ever the government's agents found him. This was why he was either incognito or absent altogether from Petrograd for long periods during the critical months in 1917. It says much for his forcefulness as party leader that despite this he continued to exercise a dominant influence over the actions of the Bolshevik Party. Trotsky later made an interesting assessment of the part played by Lenin in the October Revolution:

1 Had I not been present in 1917 in Petersburg, the October Revolution
   would still have taken place – *on the condition that Lenin was present and
   in command*. If neither Lenin nor I had been present in Petersburg, there
   would have been no October Revolution: the leadership of the
5 Bolshevik party would have prevented it from occurring.[1]

However, most historians are now careful not to overstate Lenin's power to dictate events in 1917. In the standard Bolshevik version of what happened, Lenin was portrayed as having fulfilled his plans for revolution along the lines he had laid down in such writings as his 1902 pamphlet, *What Is To Be Done?* This had visualised the development of a tightly-knit, disciplined Bolshevik Party which would seize power in the name of the masses at the opportune moment (see page 40). Yet the structure and authority of his party in 1917 were markedly different from Lenin's 1902 model. The evidence of the many disputes within the Bolshevik ranks over policy between February and October suggests that they were by no means as disciplined or centrally-controlled as the party later claimed it had been.

Part of the explanation for this is that the composition of the party had changed in ways which Lenin and the Central Committee had not planned. After the February Revolution there had been a major increase in membership which the Central Committee had not wanted but which, in the mixture of post-Revolution enthusiasm and political confusion, they seemed unable to prevent. The following figures, calculated by Western analysts, are tentative, but they do indicate the remarkable transformation which the Bolshevik Party underwent in 1917:

Membership of the Bolshevik party in 1917	
February	24,000
April	100,000
October	340,000 (60,000 in Petrograd)

Modern commentators view this influx of party members as an aspect of the general radicalisation of Russian politics that occurred as the Provisional Government got into increasing difficulties. What had helped to prepare the ground for the successful Bolshevik *coup* in October was the growth in the Petrograd factories of workers' committees which, while not necessarily pro-Bolshevik, were certainly not pro-government. One result of the anti-government agitation of these committees was that, when the open challenge to the Provisional Government came in October, Kerensky's desperate appeal for support from the people of Petrograd went unheeded.

Reference

1   Leon Trotsky, *The History of the Russian Revolution* (Gollancz, 1985) p.899

Working on Chapter 5

This chapter attempts to explain the October Revolution by reference to the key developments between February and October 1917. Those months were a period of rapid and often dramatic change. Since effective analysis depends on sound chronology, it is important when studying 1917 to acquire an understanding of the order in which events occurred. The key dates at the start of the chapter should provide a useful base on which you can build your own framework.

Answering structured and essay questions on Chapter 5

Examples of structured questions on the events of 1917:

1. Describe how Lenin's return to Petrograd in April 1917 altered the political situation there
2. Outline the main points in Lenin's April Theses
3. In what respects after April 1917 did the Bolsheviks differ from the other main political parties in Russia in their attitude towards the war with Germany?
4. Describe the difficulties encountered by Provisional Government between February and October 1917.
5. Describe the main steps by which the Bolsheviks came to power in October 1917.

The importance of the October Revolution of 1917 makes it a rich vein from which essay questions are mined. There is one question that could be said to cover everything of importance: Why did the Provisional Government fail and the Bolshevik Party succeed in 1917? However, precisely because it does cover practically everything it is highly unlikely that it would ever be set as a single question. What needs to be done, therefore, is to frame a range of questions that each

Summary Diagram
The Political Shift in 1917

Political Left	Political Centre	Political Right

The Dual Authority

Provisional Government ━━━▶

◀━━━ Petrograd Soviet

By October dominated by Bolsheviks Trotsky - chairman of MRC	By October deserted by Socialists Kerensky left without allies

The Building Blocks of Revolution

Soviet Order Number 1	Lenin's return	'April Theses'	'Bread, Peace and Land'
The failure of the summer offensive		'All Power to the Soviets'	The July Days
The Kornilov affair		Trotsky and the MRC	

contribute to building an effective response to the larger question. Three main lines of approach may be suggested. These, while not touching on every possible question, do cover the essentials.

1. *The Provisional Government and its problems* – its uncertain status – its relations with the Petrograd soviet in the Dual Authority – the war question – the land and food problem – the July Days – the Kornilov affair.

2. *Lenin and the Bolsheviks* – the 'April Theses' – 'Peace, Bread and land' – 'All Power to the Soviets' – the July Days – the October Rising.

3. *The October Revolution* – Bolshevik preparations – Provisional Government weakness – the rising itself – reasons for government collapse and Bolshevik success.

There is obviously considerable overlap and common ground between these themes and their sub-sections. The Dual Authority is a very useful central strand, connecting the status and power of the government and the Petrograd soviet, the 'April Theses', the Bolshevik policy of 'All Power to the Soviets', and the final collapse of Kerensky's government.

Questions on these central themes might include:

1. **a)** How valid is the view that 'The Provisional Government was doomed to failure from the first'?
   b) Examine the view that the Bolshevik slogans, 'Bread, Peace and Land' and 'All power to the soviets' were accurate definitions of the basic problems confronting the Provisional Government.
2. **c)** Estimate the significance of Lenin's return to Russia in April.
   d) How was it that only three months after their failure in the July Days the Bolsheviks were in a position to take power?
3. **e)** Why was there so little resistance to the Bolshevik seizure of power in October 1917?
   f) How far do you agree that in October 1917 the Bolsheviks were pushing against an open door?

A possible approach to question **2d** would be:

(1) Begin with a list of the principal developments between July and October. These should include such points as the July Days, the Kornilov affair, the increasing desertions from the front, the growing disillusionment with and within the Provisional Government regarding its failure to solve Russia's outstanding problems, and the increasing Bolshevik influence in the Petrograd soviet. *(2)* From this list you can then fashion the features of the main points of the answer. An appropriate opening would be to explain that the Bolsheviks recovered from the July Days debacle largely because the Provisional Government seemed disinclined to press home their political advantage over them. Moreover, whatever advantage the government had held was lost when the Bolsheviks were able to pose as defenders of Petrograd and the Revolution against Kornilov. *(3)* The main body of the answer should emphasise how the authority of the Provisional Government, which had always been conditional on its being able to meet the challenges facing Russia, was steadily eroded by the Petrograd soviet, in which the Bolsheviks became increasingly influential. *(4)* It would be worth stressing that the question of Bolshevik recovery cannot be considered in isolation. Indeed, it is arguable that Provisional Government decline was more significant than rising Bolshevik strength. *(5)* In this context, attention should be drawn to the misjudgement by Kerensky's government of the strength of Lenin's party. In fact, each side over-estimated the power of the other and tended to play a waiting game, fearful of exposing its own weakness. Although Trotsky's plans for a *coup* against the government had been drawn up for some time, in the event the rising was occasioned by Kerensky's attempt at a pre-emptive strike against the Bolsheviks. *(6)* Trotsky's key role as chairman of the soviet's MRC was vitally important since, in fulfilment of Lenin's long-standing aim, it enabled the Bolsheviks to dress their objectives in a soviet cloak. *(7)* In the concluding part of the answer stress should be laid on the inability of the Provisional Government either to conduct a successful

war or withdraw from it. This, together with its poor record with regard to the issues of 'bread and land', encouraged a drift to the left in Russian politics. When the challenge came in October, the Provisional Government found itself without allies. The Bolsheviks did not so much seize power as pick it up after it had been dropped. A useful quotation with which to end the essay might be: 'the Bolsheviks did not inherit a ship of state, they took over a derelict hulk'.

6 The Bolshevik Consolidation of Power 1917–21

POINTS TO CONSIDER

A key point to remember is that the successful Bolshevik rising of October 1917 marked the beginning rather than the end of the Russian Revolution. After they had taken over power the Bolsheviks under Lenin faced huge problems in trying to consolidate their hold over what had been the tsarist empire. What this chapter will consider is how the new regime under Lenin dealt with the four particularly urgent questions that confronted it from the end of 1917. The first was very simple and stark – could the Bolsheviks survive? The second question grew out the first. If they did survive how were they then to extend their control over the nation at large? The third question was whether they could negotiate a quick end to the war and lift the German occupation of western Russia. The fourth question was whether, having solved the first three, they could bring economic stability to a Russia devastated by four years of war and internal upheaval.

KEY DATES

1917
November Bolsheviks issued the Decrees on Land, on Peace, and on Workers' Control.
Elections for Constituent Assembly.
December Armistice signed at Brest-Litovsk.
Cheka created.
1918–20 Russian Civil War and foreign interventions.
War Communism.
1918
January Bolsheviks forcibly dissolved the Constituent Assembly.
Red Army established.
March Treaty of Brest-Litovsk.
June Decree on Nationalisation.
July Formation of Russian Socialist Federal Soviet Republic.
Forced grain requisitions began.
Murder of tsar and his family
September Red Terror officially introduced.
1919
March Comintern established.
Bolshevik Party renamed the Communist Party.
1920
April Invading Red Army driven from Poland.
1921
March Kronstadt Rising.

1 Introduction

From the beginning, the Bolshevik regime was engaged in a desperate struggle for survival. In their government of Russia, the Bolsheviks were working from hand to mouth. They had few preconceived plans. Before 1917 their time had been spent in preparing for revolution. Little attention had been given to the details of how affairs would be organised once this had been achieved. It had always been a Marxist belief that after the final triumph of the proletariat the state would 'wither away'. Trotsky had expressed this simple faith at the time of his appointment in 1917 as commissar for foreign affairs when he said that all that was required to be done was 'to issue a few decrees, then shut up shop and go home'. But circumstances were not to allow such a relaxed approach to government.

   Two developments obliged Lenin's government to adopt dictatorial control after 1917. One was internal, the other external, but the Bolsheviks interpreted them as part of one grand design. The internal threat took the form of a Russian civil war, fought between 1918 and 1920, in which the Bolsheviks (the Reds) were confronted by a loose combination of anti-Bolshevik forces (the Whites). The external threat came in 1918–19 with a series of military interventions in Russia by a number of foreign powers, including Britain, France, the USA and Japan.

2 The Dissolution of the Constituent Assembly

KEY ISSUE What does this event reveal about Lenin's attitude towards the exercise of power?

Lenin's objective had never been to win mass support but to create a party capable of seizing power when the political situation permitted. This was why he had refused to join a broad-front opposition movement before 1917 and why he had consistently opposed any form of co-operation with the Provisional Government. After the successful October *coup* in 1917 he was even more determined not to jeopardise the Bolsheviks' newly-won power by allowing elections to dictate the pace of revolutionary change. The results of the November 1917 election to the Constituent Assembly, therefore, presented him with an immediate problem. They revealed that the Bolsheviks had won barely a quarter of the seats.

   Lenin had originally supported the idea of a Constituent Assembly, but he now calculated that it would be impossible for his party to govern effectively alongside an assembly that was overwhelmingly non-Bolshevik. His response was simple and ruthless. In January 1918, after only one day's session, the Constituent Assembly was dissolved at

Results of the election for the Constituent Assembly, November 1917

	Votes	Seats
SRs	17,490,000	370
Bolsheviks	9,844,000	175
National minority groups	8,257,000	99
Left SRs (pro-Bolshevik)	2,861,000	40
Kadets	1,986,000	17
Mensheviks	1,248,000	16
Total	41,686,000	717

gun-point by the Red Guards. This act of violence has to be viewed in context. The Bolsheviks' hold on power was precarious. Indeed, the prospects of Bolshevik survival at all seemed slim. There was strong and widespread opposition to them inside the country, and Russia was still at war with Germany, with the Allies all set to interfere should the new Russian government contemplate making a separate peace. In such an atmosphere, the Bolsheviks were not prepared to entertain thoughts of power-sharing. Lenin justified the Bolshevik action in the following terms:

1 To hand over power to the Constituent Assembly would again be com-
   promising with the malignant bourgeoisie. The Russian Soviets place the
   interests of the toiling masses far above the interests of treacherous
   compromise disguised in a new garb. As long as behind the slogan 'All
5 power to the Constituent Assembly' is concealed the slogan 'Down with
   the Soviets', civil war is inevitable. For nothing in the world will induce
   us to surrender the Soviet power. And when the Constituent Assembly
   again revealed its readiness to postpone all the painfully urgent problems
   and tasks that were placed before it by the soviets, we told the
10 Constituent Assembly that they must not be postponed for a single
   moment. And by the will of the Soviet power, the Constituent Assembly,
   which has refused to recognise the power of the people, is dissolved.
   The Soviet Revolutionary Republic will triumph no matter what the cost.

Commenting on Lenin's attitude at this stage, Trotsky observed that 'Lenin's theoretical considerations went hand in hand with the use of sharpshooters'. He recorded a remark Lenin had made to him in private: 'The dissolution of the Constituent Assembly by the Soviet Government means a complete and frank liquidation of the idea of democracy by the idea of dictatorship.' Lenin's move caused unease among some of his own supporters. Maxim Gorky, one of the Bolshevik party's leading intellectuals, wrote at the time:

1 The best Russians have lived for almost 100 years with the idea of a
   Constituent Assembly as a political organ which could provide Russian

democracy as a whole with the possibility of freely exercising its will.
On the altar of this sacred idea rivers of blood have been spilled – and
5 now the 'people's commissars' have ordered the shooting of this
democracy.

Many foreign communists were appalled by Lenin's behaviour. Rosa
Luxemburg, a German socialist, commented bitterly:

1 To be sure, every democratic institution has its limitations. But the
remedy which Lenin and Trotsky have found, the elimination of democracy itself, is worse than the disease it is supposed to cure; for it stops up
the very living source from which alone can come the correction of all the
5 short-comings of social institutions. That source is the active, untram-
melled, energetic, political life of the broadest masses of the people.

3 The Treaty of Brest-Litovsk, 1918

> **KEY ISSUE** Why were the Bolsheviks willing to accept the
> humiliation of Russia in the Treaty of Brest-Litovsk?

There was a marked difference of attitude between Lenin and Trotsky
over the way in which the war with Germany should be ended. Lenin
wanted an immediate peace; Trotsky wanted a delay. Lenin's thinking
appears to have run along the following lines. Russia's military
exhaustion made it impossible for it to fight on successfully. If
Germany eventually won the war on both fronts it would retain the
Russian territory it now possessed. But if Germany lost the war against
the Western Allies, Russia would regain its occupied lands. In the first
eventuality, Russia would not be worse off; in the second it would
actually gain, so what point was there in pretending it could continue
the war?

Lenin's readiness to make peace with Germany was not wholly
ideological. Between 1914 and 1917 the German Foreign Office had
given substantial financial support to Lenin and the Bolsheviks in the
hope that if they achieved their revolution they would pull Russia out
of the war. Germany continued to finance Lenin even after the
October Revolution and the armistice of December 1917. A settlement with Germany was, therefore, very much in Lenin's interests
since it seemed the best guarantee against the drying up of this
considerable source of Bolshevik revenue.

Trotsky took a middle position between Lenin, who wanted an
immediate peace, and those Bolsheviks and Left Revolutionaries who
pressed for the continuation of the war as a revolutionary crusade
against imperialist Germany. Trotsky also accepted that Bolshevik
Russia had no realistic chance of continuing the military struggle
against Germany. However, in the hope that within a short time the

German armies would collapse on the Western Front and revolution would follow in Germany, he was determined to make the peace talks a protracted affair. This approach, for which he coined the slogan 'no peace, no war', was intended to confuse and infuriate the German delegation and to buy time for Bolshevik agitators to exploit the mutinies in the Austro-German armies. At Brest-Litovsk, the Polish town where the Germans and Russians gathered to discuss peace terms, Trotsky chose deliberately to embarrass and annoy the German delegation. He showed his contempt for what he called 'bourgeois propriety' by consistently flouting the accepted rules of European diplomacy. Germany's chief negotiator, Field-Marshal Hindenburg, complained:

> Trotsky degraded the conference-table to the level of a tub-thumper's street corner. Lenin and Trotsky behaved more like victors than vanquished, while trying to sow the seeds of political dissolution in the ranks of our army.

What Hindenburg had failed to grasp was that Trotsky and Lenin did indeed see themselves as victors – potential if not actual. They were not perturbed by the thought of national defeat. Their conviction was that time and history were on their side. They believed that a great international political victory was imminent. It is important to remember that Lenin and Trotsky, as international revolutionaries, had only a limited loyalty towards Russia as a nation. Their first concern was to spread the proletarian revolution.

This readiness to subordinate Russian national interests explains why, to the dismay of most Russians and many Bolsheviks, the Soviet delegation at Brest-Litovsk was eventually willing to sign a devastating peace treaty as soon as it became clear that the exasperated Germans were preparing to renew hostilities. Even so, Trotsky's outlook as an international revolutionary did not prevent him from scoring a sharp nationalist propaganda point. Before signing the treaty on 3 March 1918 Sokolnikov, the Soviet representative, declared, under instructions from Trotsky, that it was not a freely-negotiated settlement but a German *Diktat* imposed on a helpless Russia. Backing was given to this claim by the terms of the treaty, which could hardly have been more humiliating for Russia. A huge slice of territory, amounting to a third of European Russia, stretching from the Baltic to the Black Sea and including the Ukraine, Russia's major grain-source, was ceded to Germany or her allies. The land lost – about a million square kilometres – contained a population of 45 million. In addition, Russia was required to pay three billion roubles in war reparations. Aware that the signing of the treaty would be resented by many Bolsheviks, who were urging a revolutionary struggle against Germany, Lenin stressed that his policy was the only realistic one:

> Our impulse tells us to rebel, to refuse to sign this robber peace. Our reason will in our calmer moments tell us the plain naked truth – that

Russia can offer no physical resistance because she is materially
exhausted by three-years' war. It is true that there may be people who
5 are willing to fight and die in a great cause. But they are romanticists,
who would sacrifice themselves without prospects of real advantage.
Wars are won today, not by enthusiasm alone, but by technical skill,
railways, abundance of supplies. Has the Russian Revolution any of these
in the face of an enemy equipped with all the techniques of bourgeois
10 'civilisation'? The Russian Revolution must sign the peace to obtain a
breathing space to recuperate for the struggle. The central point of the
world struggle now is the rivalry between English and German finance-
capital. Let the Revolution utilise this struggle for its own ends.

Lenin's argument was a powerful one, yet he still experienced great
difficulty in convincing his colleagues. The issue was debated bitterly
in the Central Committee. In the end, Lenin gained his way only by a
majority of one in a crucial Committee division. A profound issue lay
at the base of Bolshevik disagreements. To understand this, it has to
be re-emphasised that Lenin and Trotsky were primarily international
revolutionaries. They expected workers' risings, based on the Russian
model, to sweep across Europe. Purely national conflicts would soon
be superseded by the international class struggle of the workers.
Lenin and Trotsky regarded the crippling terms of the Treaty of
Brest-Litovsk as of small account when set against the great tide of
world revolution.

Not all Bolsheviks shared this vision. A number (referred to as 'Left
Communists') were convinced that their first task was to consolidate
the October Revolution by driving out the German imperialists. It was
only Lenin's insistence on the absolute need for party loyalty in a time
of crisis that finally persuaded such Bolsheviks to subordinate their
patriotism to their ideology. Serious opposition to Lenin's leadership
might well have persisted had not the turn of military events in western
Europe saved the day. What eventually destroyed the argument of the
Left Communists and the Left SRs was the collapse of Germany's western front in August 1918, followed by the almost total withdrawal of
German forces from Russia. Lenin's gamble that circumstances would
soon make the Treaty of Brest-Litovsk meaningless had paid off. It
strengthened his hold over the party and provided the opportunity to
expel the Left SRs from the government and to outlaw them politically.

4 The Russian Civil War, 1918–20

KEY ISSUES How far was Lenin personally responsible for the
Civil War?
Was the victory of the Reds a result of their strength or the
Whites' weakness?

The Bolsheviks' crushing of the Constituent Assembly in January 1918 and their subsequent outlawing of all other parties showed that they were not prepared to share power. This claim to absolute authority by the Bolsheviks made civil war unavoidable. The researches of Dominic Lieven, a modern scholar, led him to conclude that Lenin actually wanted war in 1918:

1   The civil war did not occur by accident. In 1917 the other socialist parties, in other words the Mensheviks and Social Revolutionaries, were partly guided by their fear of and revulsion for civil war. In the winter of 1917–18 the overwhelming majority of Russians supported one or
5   other of the socialist parties. An all-socialist coalition would have made counter-revolution inconceivable, particularly since it would have rested on the only legitimate authority in Russia, namely the Constituent Assembly. Some Bolsheviks would have accepted a socialist coalition but Lenin was not one of them. The Bolshevik leader
10   rejected this course and pursued policies, which, as he well knew, made civil war inevitable.[1]

The conflict that began in the summer of 1918 was not just a matter of the Bolsheviks (the Reds) facing their political enemies (the Whites) in military struggle. From the start the Civil War was a more complex affair. The Bolsheviks presented it as a class war, but it was never simply this. The sheer size of Russia often meant that local or regional considerations predominated over larger issues. Significantly, a number of Russia's national minorities, such as the Ukrainians and the Georgians, fought in the war primarily to establish their independence from Russia. These national forces became known as the Greens. The best-known of the Green leaders was Makhno, a one-time Bolshevik, who organised a guerilla resistance to the Reds in the Ukraine.

It was ironic that, although most of the leading Bolsheviks were non-Russian, their rule was seen by many as yet another attempt to re-assert Russian authority over the rest of the country – the very situation that had prevailed under the tsars. As in all civil wars, the disruption provided a cover for settling old scores and pursuing personal vendettas, and it was not uncommon for villages or families to be divided against each other. On occasion, the fighting was simply a desperate struggle for food. Famine provided the backdrop to the Civil War. The dislocation of supplies that had occurred during the war against Germany persisted. Until this was remedied whole areas of Russia remained in a desperate economic plight.

The failure of the new regime to end hunger was an important factor in creating the initial military opposition to the Bolsheviks in 1918. In addition to the problems of a fractured transport system, Lenin's government was faced with the loss to Germany of Russia's main wheat-supply area, the Ukraine. In March 1918, the month in which the Brest-Litovsk Treaty was signed, the bread ration in

Petrograd reached its lowest ever allocation of 50 grams per day. Hunger forced many workers out of the major industrial cities. By June 1918 the workforce in Petrograd had shrunk by sixty per cent and the overall population had declined from three to two million. A visitor to the city at this time spoke of 'entering a metropolis of cold, of hunger, of hatred, of endurance'. The Bolshevik boast that October 1917 had established worker-control of Russian industry meant little now that the workers were deserting the factories in droves.

These dire circumstances encouraged open challenges to the Bolsheviks from both left and right. SRs, who had been driven from the government for their refusal to accept the Brest-Litovsk settlement, attempted to stage a *coup* in the Moscow Soviet. (In 1918 for security reasons Moscow replaced Petrograd as the capital of Soviet Russia.) This failed, but their terrorism came closer to success. Lenin narrowly survived two attempts on his life, in July and August. The second attempt, by Dora Kaplan an SR fanatic, left him with a bullet lodged in his neck, an injury which contributed to his death four years later. In their desperation at being denied any say in government, the SRs joined the Whites in their struggle against Lenin's Reds.

Armed resistance to the Bolsheviks had occurred sporadically in various parts of Russia since October 1917. What gave focus to this struggle was the behaviour in the summer of 1918 of one of the foreign armies still in Russia. A contingent of 40,000 Czechoslovak troops, who had volunteered to fight on the Russian side in the First World War as a means of gaining independence from Austria-Hungary, found themselves isolated after the Treaty of Brest-Litovsk. They formed themselves into the Czech Legion and decided to make the long journey eastwards to Vladivostok. Their aim was eventually to rejoin the allies on the western front in the hope of winning international support for the formation of an independent Czechoslovak state. The presence of this well-equipped foreign army making its way arrogantly across Russia was resented by the Bolsheviks. Local soviets began to challenge the Czech Legion and fierce fighting accompanied its progress along the trans-Siberian railway.

All this encouraged the Whites and those groups who had been dispossessed by the dissolution of the Constituent Assembly, such as the SRs and the Kadets, to come out openly against Lenin's regime. The SRs organised a number of uprisings in central Russia and established an anti-Bolshevik Volga 'Republic' at Samara. A White 'Volunteer Army', led by General Denikin, had already been formed in the Caucasus region of southern Russia from tsarist loyalists and outlawed Kadets. In Siberia, the presence of the Czech Legion encouraged the formation of a White army under Admiral Kolchak, the self-proclaimed 'Supreme Ruler of Russia'. In Estonia, another ex-tsarist general, Yudenich, began to form a White army of resistance. White units appeared in many regions elsewhere. The speed with which they arose indicated just how limited Bolshevik control was outside the cities of western Russia.

The patch-work of political, regional and national loyalties inside Russia made the Civil War a confused affair. It is best understood as a story of the Bolsheviks' resisting attacks on four main fronts, and then taking the initiative and driving back their attackers until they eventually withdrew or surrendered. Unlike the First World War, the Civil War was a war of movement, largely dictated by the layout of Russia's railway system. It was because the Bolsheviks were largely successful in their desperate fight to maintain control of the railways that they were able to keep themselves supplied, while denying the Whites the same benefit.

The reasons for the final victory of the Reds in the Civil War are not difficult to determine. The various White armies fought as separate detachments. Apart from their obvious desire to overthrow the Bolsheviks, they were not bound together by a single aim. They were unwilling to sacrifice their individual interests in order to form a united anti-Bolshevik front. This allowed the Reds to pick off the White armies separately. In the rare cases in which the Whites did consider combining, they were too widely scattered geographically to

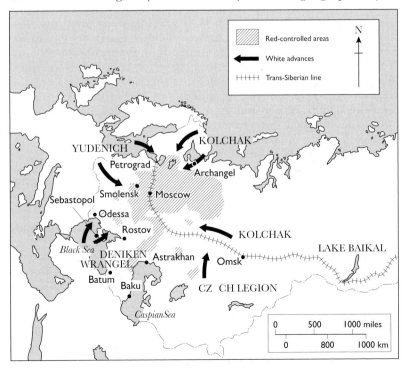

The Russian Civil War, 1918–20.

be able to bring sufficient pressure to bear on the enemy. The Reds, in contrast, remained in control of a concentrated central area of western Russia which they were able to defend by maintaining their inner communication and supply lines. The two major cities, Petrograd and Moscow, the administrative centres of Russia, remained in their hands throughout the war, as did most of the railway network. The Reds also possessed a key advantage in that the areas where they had their strongest hold were the industrial centres of Russia. This gave them access to munitions and resources denied to the Whites. The consequent dependence of the Whites on supplies from abroad appeared to prove the Red accusation that they were in league with the foreign interventionists. The Civil War had produced a paradoxical situation in which the Reds were able to stand as champions of the Russian nation as well as proletarian revolutionaries.

Although the Reds imposed a reign of terror (see page 117), the Whites were unable to capitalise on this in propaganda terms. Their own record in ill-treating local populations was as notorious as that of the Reds. To the ordinary Russian there was little to choose between the warring sides in the matter of brutality. It was not, therefore, that the Reds were genuinely popular. Indeed, by the end of the Civil War whatever initial peasant sympathy they had gained had been lost by the severity of their grain-requisitioning methods. It was that the Whites failed to present themselves as a better alternative. All they could offer was a return to the pre-revolutionary past. This was particularly damaging to them in relation to the land question. The Reds continually pointed out that all the lands which the peasants had seized in the Revolutions of 1917 would be forfeit if ever the Whites were to win the war. It was this fear more than any other that stopped the peasants from giving their support to the Whites.

Waging war is not just a matter of resources and fire-power. Morale and dedication play a vital role. Throughout the struggle the Reds were sustained by a driving sense of purpose. Trotsky as the Bolshevik war commissar may have been extreme in his methods, but he created an army which proved capable of fighting with an unshakable belief in its own eventual victory (see page 119). Set against this, the Whites were never more than an unco-ordinated group of forces, whose morale was seldom high. They were a collection of dispossessed socialists, liberals, and moderates, whose political differences often led them into bitter disputes among themselves. Save for their hatred of Bolshevism, the Whites lacked a common purpose. Throughout the Civil War, the White cause was deeply divided by the conflicting interests of those who were fighting for local separatism and those who wanted a return to strong central government. Furthermore, no White leader emerged of the stature of Trotsky or Lenin around whom an effective anti-Bolshevik army could unite.

5 The Foreign Interventions

> **KEY ISSUE** Why were the Bolsheviks able to withstand the attacks by the Allies?

When tsardom collapsed in 1917 the vital question that preoccupied the western Allies was whether the new regime would keep Russia in the war. If revolutionary Russia made a separate peace, Germany would be free to divert huge military resources from the eastern to the western front. To prevent this, the Allies offered large amounts of capital and military supplies to Russia, in return for a firm commitment from the Provisional Government to continue the war against Germany (see page 85).

The replacement of the Provisional Government by the Bolshevik regime in October 1917 had precisely the effect hoped for by Germany and feared by the Allies. Within a few weeks an armistice had been agreed between Germany and the new government, and fighting on the eastern front ceased in December 1917. The initial response of France and Britain was cautious. In the faint hope that the Bolsheviks might be persuaded to continue the fight against Germany, the same support was offered to them as to their predecessors.

Lloyd George, the British prime minister, declared that he was neither for nor against Bolshevism, but simply anti-German. He was willing to side with any group in Russia that would continue the war against Germany. However, in the circumstances prevailing in Russia, with Lenin refusing to consider a renewal of the fighting against Germany, it so happened that any help given by Britain to anti-German Russians went necessarily to anti-Bolshevik forces. It appeared to the Bolsheviks that Britain and its allies were intent on destroying them. This was matched by the Allies' view that in making a separate peace with Germany the Bolsheviks had acted as arch-traitors. The result was a fierce determination among the Allies to prevent their vital war-supplies, previously loaned to Russia and still stock-piled there, from falling into German hands

In March 1918, following the signing of the Treaty of Brest-Litovsk, British, French, and American forces occupied the ports of Murmansk in the Arctic and Archangel in the White Sea. This was the prelude to a two-year period during which armed contingents from a large number of countries occupied key areas of European, central and far-eastern Russia. These were not co-operative ventures. The declared motive of Britain, France, Germany, Italy, Japan and the USA was the legitimate protection of their individual interests. The objective of Czechoslovakia, Finland, Lithuania, Poland and Romania, all of whom directly bordered Russia, was to assert a claim, going back to tsarist times, to territorial independence from Russia. In 1918 British land forces entered Transcaucasia in southern Russia and also occupied part of central Asia. British warships entered Russian Baltic waters and the Black Sea, where they were joined by French naval vessels. The French also established a major land base around the Black Sea port of Odessa. In April 1918, Japanese troops occupied Russia's far-eastern port of Vladivostok. Four months later, they were joined by units from France, Britain, the USA and Italy. In 1919 Japanese and United States troops occupied parts of Siberia.

The Bolsheviks dismissed the claims of the interventionists simply as pretexts for an imperialist invasion of Russia to overthrow the Revolution. The Bolsheviks made no distinction between the aims of their internal enemies, the Whites, and those of the foreign interventionists. With the close of the war on the Western Front in November 1918 there was a vociferous demand from fervent anti-Bolsheviks, such as Winston Churchill, the British cabinet minister, and Marshal Foch, the French military leader, that the wartime allies should unite in a major offensive against the Bolsheviks. They pointed to the alarming spread of revolution to Germany, where in 1918–19 a short-lived Communist republic was established in Bavaria and a 'Spartacist' (Communist) rising occurred in Berlin, and also to Hungary, where early in 1919 Bela Kun led a Marxist *coup*. They also referred to the international threat posed by the creation in Moscow in 1919 of the Communist International (Comintern), the Bolshevik organisation formally dedicated to the fomenting of worldwide revolution.

There was also a key financial aspect to anti-Bolshevism in western Europe. One of the first acts of the Bolshevik regime was to declare that the new government had no intention of honouring the foreign debts of its predecessors. In addition, it nationalised a large number of foreign companies and froze all foreign assets in Russia. The bitter reaction to what was regarded as international theft was particularly strong in France where many small and middle-scale financiers had invested in tsarist Russia. It was the French who now took the lead in proposing an international campaign against the Reds.

Yet despite the preaching of an anti-Bolshevik crusade by influential voices in western Europe, no concerted attempt was made to unseat the Bolshevik regime. This was shown by the relative ease with which the interventions were resisted. The truth was that the interventionists after four long years of struggle against Germany had no stomach for a prolonged campaign. There were serious threats of mutiny in some British and French regiments when ordered to embark for Russia. Trade unionists who were sympathetic towards the new 'workers' state' refused to transport military supplies bound for Russia. Even when the foreign forces did arrive in Russia, there was seldom effective liaison between the separate national contingents. Moreover, such efforts as they made to co-operate with the White armies were half-hearted and ineffectual. The one major exception to this was in the Baltic states where the national forces, backed by British warships and troops, crushed a Bolshevik invasion and obliged Lenin's government to recognise the independence of Estonia, Latvia and Lithuania, a freedom which they maintained until taken over by Stalin in 1940.

Such success was not repeated elsewhere. After a token display of aggression, the foreign troops began everywhere to withdraw. By the end of 1919, all French and American troops had been recalled, and by the end of 1920, all other western contingents had left. It was only the Japanese who remained in Russia for the duration of the Civil War, not finally leaving until 1922. In no real sense were these withdrawals a military victory for the Bolsheviks, but that was exactly how they were portrayed in Soviet propaganda. Lenin's government presented itself as the saviour of the nation from foreign conquest. This went a considerable way to recover the esteem it had lost over the 1918 capitulation to Germany. It helped to put resolve into the waverers in the party and it lent credibility to the Bolshevik depiction of the Whites as agents of foreign powers, intent on restoring reactionary tsardom.

6 The Effects of the Civil War

> **KEY ISSUES** How did the Civil War and the foreign interventions alter Bolshevik attitudes towards international revolution?
> To what extent did the Civil War change the character of Bolshevism?

The victory of the Bolsheviks in the Civil War encouraged them to undertake what proved to be a disastrous attempt to expand their authority outside Russia. In 1920, the Red Army marched into neighbouring Poland expecting the Polish workers to rise in rebellion against their own government. However, the Poles saw the invasion as traditional Russian aggression and drove the Red Army back across the border. Soviet morale was seriously damaged, which forced Lenin and the Bolsheviks to rethink the whole question of international revolution.

Lenin adopted an essentially realistic approach. He judged that the Polish reverse, the foreign interventions in Russia, and the failure of the Communist revolutions in Germany and Hungary all showed that the time was not ripe for world revolution. The capitalist nations were still too strong. The Bolsheviks would, therefore, without abandoning their long-term revolutionary objectives, adjust their foreign policy to meet the new situation. The Comintern would continue to call for world revolution, but Soviet Russia would soften its international attitude. Lenin's concerns were very much in the tradition of Russian foreign policy. Western encroachment into Russia had been a constant fear of the tsars. That long-standing Russian worry had been increased by the hostility of European governments to the October Revolution and by their support of the Whites during the Civil War. Lenin's reading of the international situation led him to conclude that discretion was the better part of valour. Under him Soviet foreign policy was activated not by thoughts of expansion but by the desire to avoid conflict.

On the domestic front, the Civil War proved to be one of the great formative influences on the Bolshevik party (renamed the Communist Party in 1919). Their attempts to come to terms with the reality of power and learn how to govern took place in a period of conflict in which their very survival long remained in doubt. The development of the party and the government has to be set against such a background. The Revolution had been born in war, and the government had been formed in war. Of all the members of the Communist Party in 1927, a third had joined in the years 1917–20 and had fought in the Red Army. This had created a tradition of military obedience and loyalty. The Bolsheviks of this generation were hard men, forged in the fires of war.

A number of modern analysts have emphasised the central place that the Civil War had in shaping the character of Communist rule in Soviet Russia. Robert Tucker stresses that it was the military aspect of early Bolshevik government that left it with a 'readiness to resort to coercion, rule by administrative fiat, centralised administration [and] summary justice'. No regime placed in the Bolshevik predicament between 1917 and 1921 could have survived without resort to authoritarian measures. The move towards centralism in government increased as the Civil War dragged on. The emergencies of war required immediate day-to-day decisions to be made. This led to effective power moving away from the Central Committee of the Communist (Bolshevik) Party, which was too cumbersome, into the hands of the two key sub-committees, the Politburo and the Orgburo, which could act with the necessary speed. In practice, the authority of Sovnarkom, the official government of Soviet Russia, became indistinguishable from the rule of these party committees.

The centralising of authority was also evident in the official renaming in 1922 of the Soviet state as the USSR (Union of Soviet Socialist Republics). This new constitution replaced the looser Russian Socialist Federal Soviet Republic, which had been adopted in 1918. E.H. Carr observed: 'the USSR was little more than the RSFSR writ large, and represented an extension of the central authority of Moscow'.

7 The Terror

> **KEY ISSUES** Was the terror a temporary response to a desperate
> situation or an expression of Russian Communism's true
> character?
> How critical to the success of the Reds was the part played by
> Trotsky?

The repression that characterised the imposing of Bolshevik control
over Russia became known as the Terror. Some writers argue that it
was the scale of the problems confronting the Bolsheviks after the
October Revolution and the need to win a desperate civil war that
explain, and perhaps justify, the extreme measures which Lenin's
government adopted. Others assert that repression is a necessary and
unavoidable part of any political creed such as Marxism–Leninism,
which regards itself as uniquely superior to all other ideologies. A
further view is that there was something essentially totalitarian about
Lenin himself. He did not know how to act in any other way. He had
always accepted the necessity of terror as an instrument of political
control. Before 1917 he had often made it clear that a Marxist
revolution could not survive if it were not prepared to crush its
enemies:

> 1 Coercion is necessary for the transition from capitalism to socialism.
> The form of coercion is determined by the degree of development of
> the given revolutionary class, and also by special circumstances, such as,
> for example, the heritage of a long and reactionary war and the forms
> 5 of resistance put up by the bourgeoisie. Hence there is absolutely no
> contradiction between Soviet democracy and the exercise of dictatorial
> powers.

The chief instruments by which the Bolsheviks exercised their policy
of terror were the *Cheka* and the Red Army.

a) The *Cheka*

In essentials, the *Cheka* was a better organised and more efficient form
of the *Okhrana*, the tsarist secret police, at whose hands nearly every
Bolshevik activist had suffered. An idea of its purpose can be judged
from its full title, 'the All-Russian Extraordinary Commission for
Fighting Counter-Revolution, Sabotage and Speculation'. It was created in December 1917 under the direction of Felix Dzerzhinsky, an
intellectual of Polish aristocratic background who sought to atone for
his privileged origins by absolute dedication to the Bolshevik cause.
Lenin found him the ideal choice to lead the fight against the enemies of the Revolution. Dzerzhinsky never allowed finer feelings or
compassion to deter him from this task. His remorseless attitude was

shown in the various directives that issued from the *Cheka* headquarters in Moscow:

1 Our Revolution is in danger. Do not concern yourselves with the forms of revolutionary justice. We have no need for justice now. Now we have need of a battle to the death! I propose, I demand the use of the revolutionary sword which will put an end to all counter-
5 revolutionaries.

In July 1918 a group of SRs assassinated the German ambassador as a protest against the Treaty of Brest-Litovsk. A month later an attempt was made on Lenin's life (see page 110), followed by the murder of the Petrograd chairman of the *Cheka*. These incidents were made the pretext for a Bolshevik reign of terror across the greater part of Russia. It was in this atmosphere that a local *Cheka* detachment, on Lenin's personal order, executed the ex-tsar and his family in Ekaterinburg in July 1918. The summary shooting of the Romanovs without benefit of trial was typical of the manner in which the *Cheka* went about its business throughout Russia. In accordance with Dzerzhinsky's instructions, all pretence of legality was abandoned; the basic rules relating to evidence and proof of guilt ceased to exist. Persecution was directed not simply against individuals, but against whole classes. This was class war of the most direct kind:

Do not demand incriminating evidence to prove that the prisoner has opposed the Soviet government by force or words. Your first duty is to ask him to which class he belongs, what are his origins, his education, his occupation. These questions should decide the fate of the prisoner.

The savagery of the *Cheka*'s methods led to protests from within the Bolshevik party concerning the abandonment of 'socialist legality'. But there were no attempts to restrict the powers of the *Cheka*. So hazardous was the situation between 1918 and 1921 that the majority of members accepted that severe repression was necessary. The foreign interventions and the Civil War, fought out against the background of famine and imminent economic collapse, threatened to destroy the very existence of the Communist Party and the government. This had the effect of stifling criticism of the methods used to achieve survival. Dzerzhinsky was convinced that the proletarian revolution could not be saved except by 'exterminating the enemies of the working class'.

Dzerzhinsky's work was complemented by Trotsky, who used his powers as war commissar to end the independence of the trade unions which had first been legalised in 1905. Early in 1920, the workers were brought under martial discipline on the same terms as soldiers. Trotsky dismissed the unions as 'unnecessary chatterboxes' and told them: 'The working classes cannot be nomads. They must be commanded just like soldiers. This is the basis of the militarisation of labour, and without it there can be no serious talk of industrialising on new foundations'.

b) The Red Army

The creation of the Red Army was the work of Trotsky, who became commissar for war after the signing of the Treaty of Brest-Litovsk. Lenin showed his complete trust in Trotsky by giving him a wholly free hand in military matters. From his heavily-armed special train, which served as his military headquarters and travelled over vast distances, Trotsky supervised the formation and administration of a new fighting force in Russia. He had inherited 'The Workers' and Peasants' Red Army', formed early in 1918. Within two years he had turned an unpromising collection of tired Red Guard veterans and raw recruits into a formidable army of three million men. Ignoring the objections of many fellow Bolsheviks, he enlisted large numbers of ex-tsarist officers to train the rank and file into efficient soldiers. As a precaution, Trotsky attached political commissars to the army. These became an integral part of the Red Army structure. The commissars were dedicated Party workers whose function was to accompany the officers permanently and report on their political correctness. No military order carried final authority unless it was countersigned by a commissar.

Trotsky tolerated no opposition within the Red Army from officers or men. The death sentence was imposed for desertion or disloyalty. In accordance with revolutionary principles, an attempt had been made initially to dispense with the traditional forms of army discipline. Graded ranks, special uniforms, saluting and deferential titles were jettisoned as belonging to the reactionary past. However, within a short time the demands of war rendered such experiments too dangerous. Trotsky judged that tighter not looser discipline was needed. Although the term 'officer' was replaced by 'commander', in all other key respects the Red Army returned to the customary forms of rank and address, with the word 'Comrade' usually prefixing the standard terms, as in 'Comrade Captain'. The practice of electing officers, which had come into favour in the democratic atmosphere of the February Revolution, was abandoned, as were soldiers' committees.

Trotsky responded to the Civil War's increasing demand for manpower by enforcing conscription in those areas under Bolshevik control. (The Whites did the same in their areas.) Under the slogan 'Everything for the Front', Trotsky justified the severity of the Red Army's methods by referring to the dangers that Russia faced on all sides. Those individuals whose social or political background made them suspect as fighting-men were nevertheless conscripted, being formed into labour battalions for back-breaking service behind the lines. The peasants conscripted into the Red Army were for the most part reluctant warriors, and were not regarded as reliable in a crisis. Desertions were commonplace, in spite of the heavy penalties. The Bolsheviks judged that the only dependable units were those drawn predominantly from among the workers. Such units became in prac-

Photo of Lenin addressing a crowd in Moscow in May 1920. Trotsky and
Kamenev are on the steps of the podium. This photo later became
notorious when in Stalin's time it was air-brushed to remove Trotsky from it.
Despite such later attempts to deny Trotsky's role in the Revolution he had
undoubtedly been Lenin's right-hand man.

tice the elite corps or shock troops of the Red Army. Heroic stories of
the workers as defenders of the Revolution spread rapidly.

Not everything was achieved by coercion; there were idealists
among the troops who believed sincerely in the Communist mission
to create a new proletarian world. Theirs was a vital contribution to
the relatively high morale of the Reds. Although by the standards of
the European armies of the time the Red Army was deficient in
equipment and expertise, within Russia it soon came to outstrip its
White opponents in its efficiency and sense of purpose.

Throughout the Civil War, Reds and Whites continually accused
each other of committing atrocities. Both were right. Both sides did
undoubtedly use terror as a means of crushing opposition in the areas
they seized. The actual fighting seems not to have been unduly
bloody; it was in the aftermath, when the civilian population was
cowed into submission, that the savagery usually occurred. The Reds
gained recruits by offering defeated enemy troops and uncommitted
civilians the stark choice of enlistment or execution.

Trotsky's strategy was simple and direct: to defend the Red Army's internal lines of communication, to deny the Whites the opportunity to concentrate large forces in any one location, and to prevent them from maintaining regular supplies. The key to this was control of Russia's railways. Trotsky viewed the role of the railways as equivalent to that of the cavalry in former times. They were the means of transporting troops swiftly and in large numbers to the critical areas of defence or attack. It was no accident that the decisive confrontations between Reds and Whites took place near rail heads and depots. Trotsky's broad strategy was successful. Once the Reds had established an impregnable defence of their inner lines, they were able to exhaust the Whites as an attacking force and then drive them back on the major fronts until they scattered or surrendered.

Despite Trotsky's military triumphs, his authority did not go unchallenged. He met opposition from local Red commanders and commissars over tactics. His most notable dispute was with Joseph Stalin, who acted as political commissar in the Caucasus. Their legendary personal hostility dates from the Civil War days. Nonetheless, whatever the disputes, there was no doubting that Trotsky's organisation and leadership of the Red Army was the major factor in the survival of Bolshevik Russia.

8 The Kronstadt Rising, 1921

> **KEY ISSUE** In what sense was the Kronstadt Rising 'a lightning flash that lit up reality'?

The victory of the Red Army in the Civil War did not mark the end of Bolshevik coercion. The policy of war communism continued (see page 131). This involved the systematic use of terror by the *Cheka*, the spying on factory workers by political commissars, and the enforced requisitioning of peasant grain stocks. As a short-term measure it had produced the results Lenin wanted, but its severity had increased Bolshevik unpopularity. Throughout 1920 there were outbreaks of resistance, the most serious occurring in the central Russian province of Tambov. As long as unrest was confined to the peasants and to the Bolsheviks' political enemies it was a containable problem. What became deeply worrying to Lenin in 1921 was the development of opposition to war communism within the party itself. Two prominent Bolsheviks, Alexander Shlyapnikov, the labour commissar, and Alexandra Kollontai, the outstanding woman in the party, led a 'Workers Opposition' movement against the excesses of war communism. Kollontai produced a pamphlet in which she accused the party leaders of losing touch with the proletariat:

1 The workers ask – who are we? Are we really the prop of the class dictatorship, or just an obedient flock that serves as a support for those,
   who, having severed all ties with the masses, carry out their own policy
   and build up industry without any regard to our opinions and creative
5 abilities under the reliable cover of the party label.

Picking up the cue given by the 'Workers' Opposition', groups of
workers in Petrograd went on strike early in 1921, justifying their
actions in an angrily worded proclamation:

1 A complete change is necessary in the policies of the Government. First
   of all, the workers and peasants need freedom. They don't want to live
   by the decrees of the Bolsheviks; they want to control their own des-
   tinies. Comrades, preserve revolutionary order! Determinedly and in
5 an organised manner demand: liberation of all the arrested Socialists
   and non-partisan working-men; abolition of martial law; freedom of
   speech, press and assembly for all who labour.

By February 1921, thousands of Petrograd workers had crossed to the
naval base on Kronstadt. There they linked up with the sailors and
dockyard workers to demonstrate for greater freedom. They
demanded that in a workers' state, which the Bolshevik government
claimed Soviet Russia to be, the workers should be better, not worse,
off than in tsarist times. The political commissars, sent from
Petrograd by Lenin in an attempt to pacify the strikers, were greeted
with derision. Petrechenko, a spokesman for the demonstrators,
rounded on the commissars at a public meeting:

1 You are comfortable; you are warm; you commissars live in the palaces
   ... Comrades, look around you and you will see that we have fallen into
   a terrible mire. We were pulled into this mire by a group of Communist
   bureaucrats, who, under the mask of Communism, have feathered their
5 nests in our republic. I myself was a Communist, and I call on you,
   Comrades, drive out these false Communists who set worker against
   peasant and peasant against worker. Enough shooting of our brothers!

Early in March, the sailors and workers of Kronstadt elected
Petrechenko as chairman of a 15-man Revolutionary Committee,
responsible for representing their grievances to the government. This
committee produced a manifesto which included the following
demands:

1. New elections to the soviets, to be held by secret ballot.
2. Freedom of speech and of the press.
3. Freedom of assembly.
4. Rights for trade unions and release of imprisoned trade
   unionists.
5. Ending of the right of Communists to be the only permitted
   socialist political party.

6. The release of left-wing political prisoners.
7. Ending of special food rations for Communist Party members.
8. Freedom for individuals to bring food from the country into the towns without confiscation.
9. Withdrawal of political commissars from the factories.
10. Ending of the Communist Party monopoly of the press.

In responding to this manifesto, the chief concern of the Bolsheviks was not the demands themselves but their source. The workers and sailors of Kronstadt had been the great supporters of the Bolsheviks in 1917 (see page 87). Trotsky had referred to them as 'the heroes of the Revolution'. It was these same heroes who were now insisting that the Bolshevik government return to the promises that had inspired the Revolution. For all the efforts of the Bolshevik press to brand the Kronstadt protesters as White agents, the reality was that they were genuine socialists who had previously been wholly loyal to Lenin's government, but who had become appalled by the regime's betrayal of the workers' cause.

Disturbed by the growing number of strikers and their increasing demands, Trotsky ordered the Red Army under General Tukhachevsky to cross the late winter ice linking Kronstadt to Petrograd and crush 'the tools of former tsarist generals and agents of the interventionists'. An ultimatum was issued to the demonstrators. When this was rejected, Tukhachevsky gave the signal for his force, made up of Red Army units and *Cheka* detachments, to attack. After an artillery bombardment, 60,000 Red troops stormed the Kronstadt base. The sailors and workers resisted fiercely. Savage fighting occurred before they were finally overcome. Tukhachevsky reported back to Trotsky:

1 The sailors fought like wild beasts. I cannot understand where they found the might for such rage. Each house where they were located had to be taken by storm. An entire company fought for an hour to capture one house and when the house was captured it was found to contain
5 two or three soldiers at a machine-gun. They seemed half-dead, but they snatched their revolvers and gasped, 'We didn't shoot enough at you bastards.'

Immediately after the rising had been suppressed, the ring leaders who had survived were condemned as White reactionaries and shot. In the succeeding months the *Cheka* hunted down and executed those rebels who had escaped from Kronstadt. Lenin justified the severity on the grounds that the rising had been the work of the bourgeois enemies of the October Revolution: 'Both the Mensheviks and the Socialist Revolutionaries declared the Kronstadt movement to be their own.' However, as well as being a propagandist, Lenin was also a realist. He took the lesson of Kronstadt to heart. He decided it was time to lessen the rigours of war communism in order to avoid another open challenge to his party and government. At the Tenth Conference of the Communist Party, which opened in March 1921, Lenin declared that the Kronstadt rising had 'lit up reality like a lightning flash'. This was the prelude to his introduction of the New Economic Policy, a move intended to tackle the famine and in doing so to lessen the opposition to Bolshevism (see page 134). However, this was to be a purely economic adjustment. Politically, Lenin made no concessions: the screw of Communist control was turned even tighter.

Reference

1   Dominic Lieven, *Nicholas II Emperor of All the Russias* (Pimlico, 1993) p.249

Working on Chapter 6

You should aim to study the four years in question in chronological order so as to provide yourself with a sound understanding of the military, political and economic problems confronting the Bolsheviks from 1917 onwards and the ways in which they attempted to deal with them. The four key questions facing the Bolsheviks, introduced in 'Points to Consider', should be your focus.

Answering structured and essay questions on Chapter 6

Although questions vary in their style, there are three main types you are likely to face:

Structured – straightforward question that ask you to describe what happened. These usually have such openings as: 'Describe ...', 'Outline ...', 'Trace ...', 'In what ways ...?'. The emphasis is on *what* happened. You are not being asked to explain why or to make a judgement.

Causal – questions that ask you to explain *why* things happened. This usually has such openings as 'Why ...?', 'Explain ...', 'Explain why ...', 'Account for...', 'How would you account for ...'.

Judgemental – questions that ask you to make a historical judgment or assessment. These usually contain an assertion, often in quotation form, which you are then asked to consider. Typical forms of such questions are: 'How far do you agree that ...?', 'How far do you accept ...?' 'How valid is the view that ...?'

The following questions on sections 1 to 7 of this chapter offer examples of all of these types. Before you attempt any of them, check

Summary Diagram
The Bolshevik Consolidation of Power 1918–21

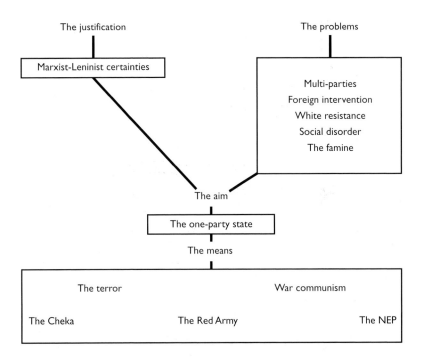

to see into which of the three category each of them fits. It is not giving too much away to say that the first question in each of the seven groupings is a structured one.

1. **a)** Describe the ways in which Lenin and the Bolsheviks responded to the results of the elections to the Constituent Assembly.
   b) Why did Lenin order the dissolution of the Constituent Assembly in 1918?
2. **a)** Outline the main points in the Treaty of Brest-Litovsk of 1918.
   b) Explain why there was disagreement among the Bolsheviks over the signing of the Treaty of Brest-Litovsk.
3. **a)** Trace the steps that led to the Russian Civil War of 1918–20.
   b) How would you account for the victory of the Reds over the Whites in the Civil War?
4. **a)** Describe the main features of the foreign interventions in Russia between 1918 and 1922.
   b) Explain why the efforts of the interventionists in Russia between 1918 and 1922 proved largely ineffectual.

5. **a)** In what ways was the Bolshevik party changed by the Russian Civil War?
   b) How far do you agree that the Civil War was 'a great formative influence on the development of the Bolshevik party'?
6. **a)** Describe the methods used by the Cheka and the Red Army in imposing the Terror on Russia.
   b) 'The Terror was not a temporary response to a desperate situation; it was an expression of the essential character of Lenin and the Bolsheviks.' How far do agree with this view?
7. **a)** Trace the development of the Kronstadt Rising of 1921 from its beginnings to its suppression
   b) Why did Lenin's government react so violently to the Kronstadt Rising of 1921?

Source-based questions on Chapter 6

1. The Dissolution of the Constituent Assembly
Study the election results on page 105, Lenin's statements on pages 105–7, and the comments of Maxim Gorky and Rosa Luxemburg on page 105–6. Answer the following questions:

a) Account for the failure of the Bolsheviks to do as well as the SRs in the elections to the Constituent Assembly, as recorded in the election returns on page 105. (5 marks)
b) According to the argument put forward in the extracts on page 105, what was Lenin's justification for the dissolution of the Constituent Assembly? (6 marks)
c) In what respects do the interpretations of democracy expressed by Gorky and Luxemburg differ from those put forward by Lenin in his justification for the dissolution of the Constituent Assembly? (8 marks)

2. The Terror
Read the extracts from Lenin's writings on page 117, and from Dzerzhinsky's directives on page 118. Answer the following questions:

a) What do you understand by the following reference: 'The form of coercion is determined by the degree of development of the given revolutionary class' (page 117, line 2). (3 marks)
b) Using your own knowledge, examine the ways in which the Cheka fulfilled Dzerzhinsky's instruction to launch a policy of 'exterminating the enemies of the working class' (page 118). (7 marks)
c) In what respects do Lenin's ideas and Dzerzhinsky's directives, as recorded in these sources, represent an ideology of terror? (10 marks)

3. The Kronstadt Rising

Study the extracts from 1) Kollontai's pamphlet (on page 122), 2) the workers' declaration (on page 122), 3) Petrochenko's speech (on page 122), and 4) from the ten demands (on pages 122–3). Answer the following questions:

a) Use the sources to show how by 1921 opposition to Bolshevik rule had developed within the Bolshevik party itself. (8 marks)
b) What changes in the character of and composition of the Bolshevik party are revealed by these sources? (10 marks)
c) Using sources 2 and 3, outline the steps which led to the Kronstadt Rising in March 1921. (10 marks)

7 The Bolsheviks and the Economy 1917–24

POINTS TO CONSIDER

In this chapter you will be studying the major features of the policies followed by Lenin and the Bolsheviks in their attempt to come to terms with the economic difficulties that confronted them after they took power in 1917. You will note that there were three distinct and consecutive periods of Bolshevik economic policy: state capitalism, which operated from November 1917 to June 1918; war communism, which was imposed between 1918 and 1921; and the New Economic Policy (NEP), which was introduced in 1921 and was still in operation when Lenin died in 1924.

KEY DATES

1917
November Bolsheviks issued the Decrees on Land, Peace, and
             Workers' Control.
             'State Capitalism' adopted as Bolshevik economic policy.
1918
June   War Communism superseded 'State Capitalism'.
1921
March   Introduction of the New Economic Policy (NEP).
             Decree against factionalism.
1922–3   Lenin suffered a number of increasingly severe strokes.
1922
December Soviet state became the USSR.
             Lenin completed his 'testament', critical of all the leading
             Bolsheviks.
1923
October   The Scissors Crisis.
1924
21 January Death of Lenin

The three major stages of economic policy should not be thought of as an ordered, planned progression. Throughout the period, the Bolsheviks struggled to retain control of an economic situation for which their training as revolutionaries had not prepared them. As with government and administration, they had to learn the skills of economic management as they went along. Few neutral historians now accept the traditional Soviet view that under Lenin's inspired guidance the revolutionary government after 1917 embarked on a measured transformation of the old Russian economy into a planned socialist system. Lenin's policy is now seen as having been a matter of adjustment to the harsh realities of the economic situation.

1 State Capitalism 1917–18

> **KEY ISSUE** Was Bolshevik economic policy ever anything more
> than a set of fragmented responses to a series of desperate
> situations?

The Bolsheviks inherited severe economic problems in 1917. In
theory, the October Revolution had marked the victory of proletarian
socialism over bourgeois capitalism, but theory was of little immediate
assistance in the circumstances of late 1917. Before the October
Revolution, Lenin had written powerfully against landlords and grasping capitalists, but he had produced little in the way of genuine economic planning. It is understandable, therefore, that his policy after
taking power in 1917 was a pragmatic one. He argued that the change
from a bourgeois to a proletarian economy could not be achieved
overnight. The Bolshevik government would continue to use the
existing economic structures until the transition had been completed
and a fully-fledged socialist system could be adopted. This transitional
stage was referred to as 'state capitalism'. Lenin justified it to his colleagues in the following terms:

1 Without the guidance of specialists, no transition to socialism is possible, because, as compared with capitalism, socialism requires a deliberate and forward mass movement towards higher productivity of labour.
   But the majority of specialists are bourgeois. For the present we shall
5 have to adopt the old bourgeois method and agree to pay higher
   salaries for the 'services' of the biggest bourgeois specialists. All who
   are familiar with the situation see the necessity of such a measure,
   though not all understand its significance for the proletarian state.
   Clearly it is a compromise measure.

Lenin was aware that there were many Bolsheviks who wanted the
immediate introduction of a more sweeping revolutionary policy, but
he pointed out that the new regime simply did not possess the power
to impose it. Its authority did not run much beyond Petrograd and
Moscow. Until the Bolsheviks could exercise a much wider political
and military control, their economic policy would have to fit the prevailing circumstances. The war against Germany and Austria had
brought Russia to the point of economic collapse. The shortage of
raw materials and investment capital had reduced industrial production to two-thirds of its 1914 level. Inflation had reached uncontrol-
lable heights. The transport system had been crippled, and grain
supplies were over 13 million tons short of the nation's needs. Within
a few months of the October Revolution, the food crisis had been further deepened by the ceding to Germany of the Ukraine, Russia's
richest grain-producing region (see page 107).
   All Lenin's economic policies from 1917 until his death in 1924

can be seen as a response to the basic question: how could Russia feed itself? Lenin was a realist on the peasant question. Although he considered that the future lay with the industrial workers, he was very conscious that the peasantry, who made up the mass of the population, were the food producers. The primary consideration, therefore, was how best the peasants could be persuaded or forced to provide adequate food supplies for the nation.

Immediately after coming to power, the new government introduced two measures which are usually regarded as having initiated Bolshevik economic policy. These were the 'Decree on Land' and the 'Decree on Workers' Control', both issued in November 1917. However, these were not so much new departures as formal recognitions of what had already occurred. The key article of the land decree stated:

> 1 Private ownership of land shall be abolished for ever; land shall not be sold, purchased, leased, mortgaged, or otherwise alienated. All land, whether state, crown, monastery, church, factory, entailed, private, public, peasant, etc, shall be confiscated without compensation and
> 5 become the property of the whole people, and pass into the use of all those who cultivate it.

The decree gave Bolshevik sanction to what had happened in the countryside since the February Revolution: in many areas the peasants had overthrown their landlords and occupied their property. Lenin had earlier accepted this when he had adopted the slogan 'Land to the Peasants' (see page 90). The Decree on Workers' Control was also largely concerned with authorising what had already occurred. During 1917 a large number of factories had been taken over by the workers. The workers' committees that were formed seldom ran the factories efficiently. The result was a serious fall in industrial output. The decree attempted to recognise the legitimacy of the workers' takeover, while at the same time asserting the need for discipline and order in the workplace:

> At all enterprises the owners and the representatives of the wage and salary earners elected to exercise workers' control are declared answerable to the state for the maintenance of the strictest order and discipline and for the protection of property.

The relative powerlessness of the Bolshevik government at this early stage was shown by the statistic that, for every factory formally nationalised under the decree, four more were seized by the workers without government approval being sought. One of the problems for the government was that not all the workers' committees were dominated by Bolsheviks. Until the party gained greater control at shop floor level it would be difficult for the central government to impose its will upon the factories. Nevertheless, the government pressed on with its plans for establishing the framework of state direction of the economy, even if the reality of effective central control was some way off. In December, the Supreme Council of the National Economy (*Vesenkha*) was set up 'to take charge of all existing institutions for the regulation of economic life'.

Initially, *Vesenkha* was unable to exercise the full authority granted to it. However, it did preside over a number of important developments. In 1920 a special State Commission (GOELRO) was established to organise a nationwide system for generating electricity. At the time, Lenin remarked that GOELRO was an example of his belief that 'Communism equals Soviet power, plus electrification'. The banks and the railways were nationalised, foreign debts were cancelled, and attempts were made to bring some order to the chaotic transport system. These were important practical achievements, which suggested how effective centralised economic control might become once the Bolshevik regime had gained real power.

2 War Communism 1918–21

> **KEY ISSUE** Why were there deep disagreements among the Bolsheviks over the policy of war communism?

In the summer of 1918, Lenin abruptly abandoned state capitalism and began to introduce a series of harshly restrictive economic measures, which were collectively known as 'war communism'. The chief reason for the new departure was the desperate situation created by the Civil War. Lenin judged that the fight for survival necessitated oppressive policies. The White menace could be met only by an intensification of authority in those regions which the Reds controlled (approximately 30 of the 50 provinces of European Russia). The change in economic strategy has to be seen, therefore, as part of the terror which the Bolsheviks operated in these years (see page 117). Every aspect of life, social, political and economic had to be subordinated to the task of winning the Civil War.

a) Industry

The first step towards war communism as a formal policy was taken in June 1918. Even before that date, the instruments by which it would be imposed had become available. The existence of the *Cheka* and the Red Army enabled Lenin to embark on a policy of centralisation, knowing that he had the means of enforcing compliance. By that time also, there had been a considerable increase in Bolshevik influence in the factories. This was a result of the infiltration of the workers' committees by political commissars. This development helped prepare the way for the issuing of the Decree on Nationalisation in June 1918, which within two years brought practically all the major industrial enterprises in Russia under central government control.

However, nationalisation of itself did nothing to increase production. It was imposed at a time of severe industrial disruption, which had been caused initially by the strains of the war of 1914–17 but which worsened during the Civil War. Military needs were given priority, thus denying resources to those industries not considered essential. Even where supplies were restored, the dislocated transport system prevented their effective distribution.

The situation was made more serious by the factories' being deprived of adequate manpower. This was a result both of conscription into the Red Army and of the flight from the urban areas of large numbers of inhabitants, who left either in search of food or to escape the Civil War. The populations of Petrograd and Moscow dropped by a half between 1918 and 1921. The problems for industry were deepened by hyper-inflation. The scarcity of goods and the government's policy of continuing to print currency notes effectively destroyed the value of money. By the end of 1920, the rouble had fallen to one per cent of its worth in 1917. In 1921, train and tram fares were nominally one million times higher than in 1917. Such figures quickly became meaningless and money ceased being used. Bartering became a substitute. But while the exchange of goods worked reasonably successfully on a small scale, it could not be adapted effectively to large-scale enterprise. All this meant that while war communism tightened the Bolshevik grip on industry it did not lead to economic growth. The table below shows the failure of war communism in economic terms.

	1913	1921
Index of gross industrial output	100	31
Index of large-scale industrial output	100	21
Electricity (million Kwhs)	2,039	520
Coal (million tons)	29	8.9
Oil (million tons)	9.2	3.8
Steel (million tons)	4.3	0.18
Imports (at 1913 rouble value (millions)	1,374	208
Exports (at 1913 rouble value (millions)	1,520	20

b) Agriculture

For Lenin, the major purpose of war communism was to force the peasants to provide more food. But the peasants proved difficult to bring into line. As a naturally conservative class, they were resistant to central government, whether tsarist or Bolshevik. A myth was created by the Bolsheviks that there was a class of rich peasants (known as *kulaks*) who were hoarding their grain stocks in order to keep prices artificially high. The reality was that the *kulaks* were not a separate class but were simply the more efficient farmers who were marginally more prosperous. Nor was there grain hoarding. It was rather that the peasants saw no return for themselves in being more productive until the government, which had become the main grain purchaser, was willing to pay a fair price for it. However, exasperated by the peasants' refusal to conform, the government condemned them as counter-revolutionaries and resorted to coercion. Cheka units were sent into the countryside to take the grain by force. In August 1918, the people's commissar for food issued the following orders:

1   All Soviets of Workers' and Peasants' Deputies, all committees of the poor, all trade union organisations of workers are to form immediately harvesting and grain requisition detachments. The tasks of the above-mentioned detachments are to: harvest winter grain in former landlord-
5   owned estates; harvest grain on the land of notorious *kulaks*; every food requisition detachment is to consist of not less than 75 men and two or three machine guns. The political commissar's duties are to ensure that the detachment carries out its duties and is full of revolutionary enthusiasm and discipline.

What the orders amounted to was an official promotion of violence. Between 1918 and 1921, the requisition squads systematically terrorised the countryside. The *kulaks* were targeted for particularly brutal treatment. Lenin ordered that they were to be 'mercilessly suppressed'. In a letter of 1920 that came to light in the 1990s he gave instructions that one hundred *kulaks* were to be hanged in public in order to terrify the population 'for hundreds of miles around'.

Yet the result was largely the reverse of the one intended. Even less food became available. Knowing that any surplus would simply be confiscated, the peasant produced only the barest minimum to feed himself and his family. Nevertheless, throughout the period of war communism, the Bolsheviks persisted in their belief that grain hoarding was the basic problem. Official reports continued to speak of 'concealment, concealment everywhere, in the hopes of selling grain to town speculators at fabulous prices'.

By 1921, the fall in food supplies, caused by a combination of requisitioning, drought and the general disruption of war, had created a national famine. The grain harvests in 1920 and 1921 produced less than half that gathered in 1913. Even *Pravda* admitted in 1921 that one in five of the population was starving. Matters became so desperate that the Bolsheviks, while careful to blame the *kulaks* and the Whites for the situation, were prepared to admit there was a famine and to accept foreign assistance. A number of countries supplied Russia with aid. The outstanding contribution came from the USA in the form of the American Relief Association (ARA). Notwithstanding such efforts, foreign help came too late to prevent mass starvation. Of the ten million fatalities of the Civil War period, over half starved to death.

What is now known is that Lenin positively welcomed the famine as providing an opportunity to pursue his destruction of the Orthodox Church. In a letter of 1922 he ordered the Politburo to exploit the famine by shooting priests, 'the more, the better'. He went on:

1 It is precisely now and only now when in the starving regions people are eating human flesh and hundreds if not thousands of corpses are littering the roads that we can (and therefore must) carry out the confiscation of the church valuables with the most savage and merciless
5 energy.

By 1921, the grim economic situation had undermined the original justification for war communism. During its operation, industrial and agricultural production had fallen alarmingly. This did not mean the policy necessarily became unpopular among the Bolsheviks themselves. Indeed, there were many in the party who, far from regarding it as a temporary measure to meet an extreme situation, believed that it represented true revolutionary Communism. The leading economic theorists in the party, Bukharin and Preobrazhensky, who were referred to as 'Left Bolsheviks', urged that war communism should be retained as the permanent economic strategy of the Bolshevik government. They saw the centralising of industry, the ending of private ownership, and the squeezing of the peasants as the correct application of socialist principles.

Lenin himself clung to the policy as long as he could. As late as December 1920, he was still urging that grain requisitioning should be continued. However, the failure of the economy to recover and the scale of the famine led him to consider possible alternatives to war communism. He was finally convinced of the need for change by widespread anti-Bolshevik risings in 1920–1. These were a direct reaction against the rigours of the government's policy. Lenin described these risings as illuminating the true situation like a flash of lightning (see page 124). He responded by introducing the New Economic Policy (NEP) at the Tenth Party Congress in March 1921.

3 The New Economic Policy (NEP)

> **KEY ISSUES** Was the introduction of NEP a betrayal of Communist principles?
> How far did NEP meet Russia's needs?

As with the policy it replaced, the NEP was intended by Lenin primarily to meet Russia's urgent need for food. Whatever the purity of the revolutionary theory behind war communism, it had clearly failed at a practical level. State-directed terror had not forced the peasants into producing larger grain stocks. Lenin judged, therefore, that if the peasants could not be coerced they must be persuaded. He told the delegates at the 1921 Party Congress:

1 We must try to satisfy the demands of the peasants who are dissatis-
   fied, discontented, and cannot be otherwise. In essence the small
   farmer can be satisfied with two things. First of all, there must be a certain amount of freedom for the small private proprietor; and, secondly,
5 commodities and products must be provided.

Disagreements within the Bolshevik Party over the NEP would emerge later, but in the spring of 1921 the famine and the depressed economic situation in Russia led the delegates to give unanimous support to Lenin's proposals. The decree making the NEP official government policy was published in 1921. Its essential features were the abandonment of state requisitioning and the re-introduction of the market economy, which allowed the peasants to trade for private profit.

> **KEY FEATURES** of the NEP
> – relaxing of central economic control
> – abandonment of requisitioning and its replacement by a tax in
>   kind
> – peasants allowed to keep their food surpluses and sell them for
>   a profit
> – markets were restored
> – money was restored

Lenin was aware that the new policy marked a retreat from the principle of state control of the economy. It restored a mixed economy in which capitalism existed alongside socialism. Aware of the unease of many Bolsheviks over this, Lenin was at pains to stress that the NEP was only a temporary concession to capitalism. He emphasised that the party still retained control of 'the commanding heights of the economy', by which he meant large-scale industry, banking and foreign trade. He added that he was prepared 'to let the peasants have their little bit of capitalism as long as we keep the power'
   The adoption of the NEP showed that the Bolshevik government since 1917 had been unable to restructure the Russian economy along purely ideological lines. Lenin admitted this. He told party members that it made no sense for Bolsheviks to pretend that they could pursue an economic policy which took no account of the circumstances.
   Lenin's realism demanded that political theory take second place to economic necessity. It was this that troubled the members of the party, such as Trotsky and Preobrazhensky, who had regarded the repressive measures of war communism as the proper revolutionary strategy for the Bolshevik Party to follow. They were disturbed by the concessions to the peasantry and the re-emergence of capitalism.

Trotsky described the NEP as 'the first sign of the degeneration of Bolshevism'. A main complaint of the objectors was that the reintroduction of money and private trading was creating a new class of 'Nepmen'. This was a scornful reference to those who stood to gain from the capitalism permitted under the new policy: the *kulaks*, the retailers, the traders, and the small manufacturers. It was the profiteering 'Nepmen' whom Victor Serge, a representative of the Left Bolsheviks, had in mind when he described the immediate social effects of the NEP: 'the cities we ruled over assumed a foreign aspect; we felt ourselves sinking into the mire. Money lubricated and befouled the entire machine just as under capitalism'.

The NEP was such a contentious issue among the Bolsheviks that Lenin took firm steps to prevent the party being split over it. At the Tenth Party Congress in 1921, at which the NEP had been formally announced, he introduced a resolution 'On Party Unity'. The key passage read:

1 The Congress orders the immediate dissolution, without exception, of all groups that have been formed on the basis of some platform or other, and instructs all organisations to be very strict in ensuring that no manifestations of factionalism of any sort be tolerated. Failure to
5 comply with this resolution of the Congress is to entail unconditional and immediate expulsion from the party.

The object of this proposal was to prevent groups or 'factions' within the party from criticising government or Central Committee decisions. An accompanying resolution condemned the Workers' Opposition, a group which had opposed the excesses of war communism and which had been involved in the Kronstadt Rising (see page 121). The two resolutions on party loyalty provided a highly effective means of stifling criticism of the NEP.

At the same time as Lenin presented these strictures on party factionalism, he also declared that all political parties other than the Bolsheviks were now outlawed in the USSR. 'Marxism teaches that only the Communist Party is capable of training and organising a vanguard of the proletariat and the whole mass of the working people.' This was the logical climax of the policy, begun in 1918, of suppressing all opposition to Bolshevik rule. The value to Lenin of his announcement at this critical juncture was that it made it extremely difficult for doubting members to suggest openly that the NEP threatened the supremacy of the party.

Another factor preserving Bolshevik cohesion was the decision by Bukharin, the outstanding Left Bolshevik economist, to abandon his opposition to the new policy and become its most enthusiastic supporter. His new approach was expressed in his appeal to the peasants: 'Enrich yourselves under the NEP'. Bukharin believed that the increased purchasing power of the peasants, which would result from the sale of their surplus grain, would also stimulate industry. It is significant that during the final two years of Lenin's life, when he was incapacitated by a series of crippling strokes, it was Bukharin who was his closest colleague. The last two articles published under Lenin's name, 'On Co-operation' and 'Better Fewer, But Better', were justifications of the NEP. Both were the work of Bukharin.

In the event, the most powerful reason for the party to accept the NEP proved to be a statistical one. The production figures suggested that the policy worked. By the time of Lenin's death, the Soviet economy had begun to make a marked recovery. The table below indicates the scale of the growth in output and in wages.

	1921	1922	1923	1924	1925
Grain harvest (million tons)	37.6	50.3	56.6	51.4	72.5
Value of factory output (in millions of roubles)	2004	2619	4005	4660	7739
Electricity (million Kwhs)	520	775	1146	1562	2925
Average monthly wage of urban worker (in roubles)	10.2	12.2	15.9	20.8	25.2

4 Conclusion

Lenin's claim that under the NEP the Bolsheviks would still control 'the commanding heights of the economy' was shown to be substantially correct by the census of 1923. The figures indicated that, in broad terms, the NEP had produced an economic balance: while agriculture and trade were largely in private hands, the state dominated Russian industry.

Share of Trade	
Private traders ('Nepmen')	75%
The State	15%
Co-operatives	10%

	Proportion of industrial workforce	Average number of workers in each factory
Private enterprises	12%	2
State enterprises	85%	155
Co-operatives	3%	15

The NEP was not a total success. Its opponents criticised it on the grounds that the balance it appeared to have achieved was notional rather than real. The fact was that industry failed to expand as fast as agriculture. The 'Nepmen' may have done well, but there was high

Index of prices – 100 in 1913

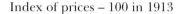

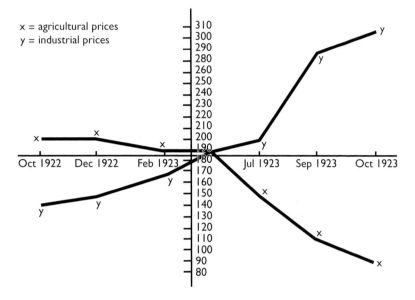

The 'Scissors Crisis'.

unemployment in the urban areas. The disparity between agricultural and industrial growth rates had led by 1923 to a situation that became known as the 'Scissors Crisis'. This was the figurative way in which Trotsky, at the Twelfth Party Congress in that year, likened the problem created by the widening gap between industrial and agricultural prices to the open blades of a pair of scissors.

Ironically, the crisis was caused in part by the revival of agriculture and the ending of the famine. In 1922 and 1923, kinder weather and an increase in the amount of land under cultivation produced greater harvests, which then led to a fall in the price of food. However, this was not matched by a comparable drop in the price of industrial goods. Factories took much longer than the land to recover from the chaos of the Civil War, and were unable to meet the growing demand for manufactured goods. The scarcity of factory products drove up their price at the same time as the increased amount of food available was reducing the cost of agricultural products. The net result was that the peasants found that they were having to sell their produce at too low a price for them to be able to afford the inflated cost of manufactured goods. This resurrected the very problem that had originally led Lenin to adopt NEP – the danger that the peasants would lose their incentive to produce surplus food. Should this recur, the Russian economy overall would return to the depressed condition of the war communism period.

With Lenin's illness restricting him from playing an effective political role, divisions within the party re-emerged. Trotsky declined to serve on a special 'Scissors Committee' set up by the Central Committee at the height of the crisis in October 1923. Instead, he became the spokesman of 'the Platform of 46', a group of 46 party members who issued an open letter condemning the government's 'flagrant radical errors of economic policy' which had subordinated Soviet Russia's needs to the interests of the 'Nepmen'. Trotsky's arguments were strengthened by the undeniable failure of *Vesenkha* (renamed *Gosplan* in 1921) to formulate a national economic strategy. *Gosplan* issued a number of impressive-sounding pronouncements, but it achieved little in the practical field. After three years its chairman had to admit that Soviet Russia still lacked 'a single economic plan'.

A confrontation between supporters and critics of NEP was averted for the time being by an upturn in the economy. After October 1923 the retail price of industrial goods began to fall from the critically high level of that month. Industry continued to recover and an abundant harvest guaranteed the maintenance of food supplies. The blades of the scissors began to close. By 1924, industry had largely recovered from the depression into which it had sunk before the introduction of the NEP in 1921.

Yet these were only temporary gains; they were no guarantee of permanent economic or political stability. The question of how long the NEP would continue to operate and whether it genuinely represented the aspirations of the Soviet state remained unsettled at the time of Lenin's death in 1924. The period from 1917 to 1924 had shown the wide gap between revolutionary theory and economic reality. It could be argued that Bolshevik policy in these years, far from being a matter of structured economic planning, was never anything more than a set of fragmented responses to a series of desperate situations.

Working on Chapter 7

Concentrate on gaining an understanding of the major economic developments in the period by following the pattern of analysis that appears in the chapter. In Russian history there has always been a very considerable overlap between political and economic affairs. This is particularly true of the period 1917–24, so it would help if you made cross references to chapter 6 on such issues as the NEP, for example. It is unlikely that you would be asked exam questions on technical economic matters but you would need to show that you understood that it was economic pressures that largely explain why the Bolsheviks behaved the way they did between 1917 and 1924. The political aspects of the NEP are likely to remain a popular theme with examiners.

Answering structured and essay questions on Chapter 7

1. Describe the main economic problems faced by Lenin's government between 1917 and 1924.
2. Describe the ways in which the Bolsheviks tried to deal with the problem of food supplies in Russia between 1918 and 1924.
3. Describe the main features of War Communism as developed by the Bolsheviks under Lenin.
4. In what ways did the NEP reverse the policy of War Communism?
5. Why did Lenin consider it necessary to introduce the NEP in 1921?
6. How would you account for the serious division of opinion among the Bolsheviks over the NEP?
7. How far do you agree that the introduction of the NEP marked 'a betrayal of Bolshevism'?
8. Do you agree that by 1924 the NEP had largely fulfilled the objectives Lenin had had when introducing it in 1921?
9. How valid is the view that the economic policies followed by Lenin and the Bolsheviks after 1917 'turned Marxism on its head'?

Consider question 7. This is a good test of how well you have understood the link between politics and economics. You would do well to begin by defining what you regard as the essential features of Bolshevism. List the political and economic aspects of this. To put matters into perspective you will need to spend some time on War Communism, explaining that for some die-hard Bolsheviks the rigours of that policy were perfectly in keeping with the party's true aim of destroying their social and political enemies and overthrowing capitalism in order to create a Communist state. This is where the concept of the NEP as betrayal becomes central. To Bolsheviks who thought that way, Lenin's resort to the NEP was a return to capitalism and put the Revolution at risk. Here you need to give your judgement on whether they were right or whether Lenin's claim that the NEP was purely an expedient and temporary measure showed his realism. You should give consideration to Lenin's fierce determination not to allow NEP to be the occasion for any weakening of Bolshevik control on the political front.

Sourced-based questions on Chapter 7

1. War Communism

Study the data on page 132, the requisition order on page 133, and then answer the following questions:

a) Using your own knowledge, suggest reasons for the difference between the indices of industrial output for 1913 and 1921. (5 marks)

b) Explain the meaning of the term 'notorious *kulaks*' as used in the extract on page 133, line 5. (3 marks)

c) In the light of the evidence in the requisition order, comment on the judgment that the methods of collecting grain amounted to 'an official policy of violence'. (8 marks)

d) Of what value are these two sources to the historian studying the nature of war communism? (10 marks)

2. The NEP

Study Lenin's statement on page 135, the resolution on page 136, and the tables on page 137. Answer the following questions:

a) Using your own knowledge and the evidence in Lenin's statement, explain why Lenin introduced the NEP in 1921. (6 marks)

b) Using you own knowledge, expalin why Lenin was so determined that the Tenth Party Congress should adopt the resolution On Party Unity. (6 marks)

c) Examine the strengths and limitations of the table on page 137 as evidence of the effect of the NEP on the Soviet economy. (7 marks)

d) How far does the table on page 137, showing the distribution of trade and industry, suggest that the NEP had produced an economic balance between private and state industry? (8 marks)

e) Using all these sources and your own knowledge, trace the development of the NEP between 1921 and 1924. (10 marks)

8 Conclusion

POINTS TO CONSIDER

The conclusion surveys the years 1881–1924 and offers three main arguments: 1 – that despite the upheavals of war and revolution there is a strong continuity in the Russian history of this period; 2 – that the Bolshevik *coup* in October 1917 did not mark a real break with the past, since, although the form of government changed, its essentially authoritarian and non-representative character remained; 3 – that the October Revolution was not a victory for Marxism, since Lenin in his leadership and consolidation of the Revolution did not follow or fulfil strict Marxist theory. You are invited to examine these propositions to see how far they match your understanding of the siginificance of this period. There is a last section describing the major interpretations of the Russian Revolution. You should find this helpful if you are interested in learning how views of this critical period have developed since 1917.

1 The Continuity of Russian History 1881–1924

> **KEY ISSUE** Why had Russia been unable to modernise itself fully in this period?

In 1881 reformers and revolutionaries were in agreement that Russia had to be modernised. On occasions, as under Witte's and Stolypin's leadership, tsardom dallied with the idea of reform. But too often reaction prevailed. In the end the tsarist system showed itself unwilling to make the political adjustments needed to accommodate the social and economic changes that were occurring. It seemed to have overcome the challenge of 1905, but later events suggested this had been no more than a reprieve. Whether tsardom would have survived but for the onset of war in 1914 must remain an open question, but the fact was that the war revealed both the fragility of the economic advance that had been achieved since the 1890s and the administrative weakness of the tsarist state. The war also finally destroyed the myth of the tsar as providential protector of the Russian people. The incapacity of Nicholas II in the face of the military and political crises that confronted Russia after 1914 eroded the loyalty of the Russian people. By February 1917 not even the tsar's traditional supporters were prepared to save him. It was not the demonstrators in Petrograd, but the army high command and the aristocratic members of the duma who advised him to abdicate.

The collapse of tsardom left a power vacuum which the Provisional Government proved unable to fill. The reconstituted duma which succeeded the tsar in February held office, but it never held power. It lacked the ruthlessness which the desperate situation demanded. From the first, its authority was weakened by the existence of the Petrograd Soviet. Unable to fight the war successfully and unwilling to introduce the social reforms that might have given it a popular base, the Provisional Government tottered towards collapse. When it was challenged in October 1917 by the Bolsheviks, who themselves had been on the point of political extinction in July, it was friendless. It gave in with scarcely a show of resistance. In name, it was the soviets which then took power, but in reality it was the Bolsheviks, who proceeded to turn Russia into a one-party-state. It took them three years of bitter civil war to do it, but they alone of all the political parties in post-revolutionary Russia had the necessary ruthlessness to destroy whatever stood in their way.

Although Lenin rejected the Russian past, he remained very much its heir. He had as little time for democracy as the tsars had. The rule of the Bolsheviks was a continuation of the absolutist tradition in Russia. The Civil War and the foreign interventions, by intensifying the threat to the Bolshevik government, provided it with the pretext for demanding total conformity from the masses and the party members as the price of the Revolution's survival. Yet it is doubtful whether, even without that threat, Bolshevism could have developed other than as an oppressive system. Its dogmatic Marxist creed made it as intolerant of other political ideas as tsardom had been. The forcible dissolution of the Constituent Assembly in 1918, the Terror, and the crushing of the Kronstadt revolt in 1921 were clear proof of the absolutism of Bolshevik control. 1917 did not mark a complete break with the past. Rather it was the replacement of one form of state authoritarianism with another.

2 Lenin's Role as a Revolutionary

> **KEY ISSUE** What principles guided Lenin as a revolutionary?

Lenin's greatest single achievement as a revolutionary was to reshape Marxist theory to make it fit Russian conditions. The instrument which he chose for this was the Bolshevik Party. Although Lenin was careful always to describe his policies as democratic, for him the term had a particular meaning. Democracy was not to be reckoned as a matter of numbers but as a method of Party rule. Because the party was the vehicle of historical change, its role was not to win large-scale backing but to direct the Revolution from above, regardless of the scale of popular support. 'No revolution', Lenin wrote, 'ever waits for formal majorities'.

Lenin's political certainties followed logically from his view of the contemporary Russian working class. Its small size and limited political awareness meant that it could not achieve revolution unaided. It was, therefore, the historical mission of the enlightened Bolshevik Party to use its understanding of the scientific principles governing human society to guide the proletariat towards its revolutionary destiny. Since authority emanated from the centre outwards, it was the role of the leaders to lead, the role of the party members to follow. The special term describing this was 'democratic centralism'. Lenin defined it in these terms:

1 Classes are led by parties, and parties are led by individuals who are called leaders. This is the ABC. The will of a class is sometimes fulfilled by a dictator. Soviet socialist democracy is not in the least incompatible with individual rule and dictatorship. What is necessary is individual
5 rule, the recognition of the dictatorial powers of one man. All phrases about equal rights are nonsense.

A marked feature of Lenin as a revolutionary was his ability to adjust theory to fit circumstances. This pragmatic approach often led him to diverge from the strict pattern of the Marxist dialectic with its clear-cut stages of class revolution, but it made him and his followers infinitely adaptable. In his writings and speeches he always insisted that his ideas were wholly in accordance with those of Marx. However, in practical terms, Lenin's role in Russia after April 1917 was that of a skilled opportunist who outmanoeuvred a collection of opponents who never matched him in sense of purpose and sheer determination.

Lenin introduced the notion of 'the telescoped revolution', which asserted that the final two stages of revolution, bourgeois and proletarian, could be compressed into one. This would allow the Bolsheviks to organise revolution against the Provisional Government without having to wait for the Russian proletariat to grow substantially in size. It would not be necessary for the Russian workers to initiate the Revolution; it would be enough that it would be carried out in their name by the Bolsheviks, the special instruments of historical change and the true voice of the proletariat. This readiness to make Marxist theory conform to practical necessity was very evident in Lenin's economic policies. A basic premise of Marxism was that political systems were determined by the economic structure on which they rested. Lenin turned this idea upside down. His government after 1917 used its political power to determine the character of the economy. His flexible approach was then shown in 1921 when he introduced the NEP, a policy that entailed the abandonment of war communism and a reversion to capitalism.

Lenin was perfectly clear about what his ultimate objectives were and he was untroubled by the harsh methods he employed to achieve them. The end justified the means. This approach was wholly consistent with his interpretation of the scientific nature of Marxism. Once the concept of the historical inevitability of the proletarian revolution had been accepted, it followed that the binding duty of revolutionaries was to work for that end by whatever means necessary. It was a Marxist principle that morality was not a set of universal values but was simply the method by which the ruling class of the day imposed its control. Before the Revolution, bourgeois morality had been used to oppress the workers. After the Revolution, socialist morality was being used to oppress the reactionaries. In such circumstances violence was perfectly legitimate. The only question was whether its use advanced or retarded revolution. The Terror enforced by Lenin during the Civil War period rested upon this particular concept of conditional morality. He told the Komsomol (Young Communists) Congress in 1920:

1 We say that our morality is entirely subordinated to the interests of the proletariat's class struggle. Morality is what serves to destroy the old exploiting society and to unite all the working people around the proletariat, which is building a new, a communist society. To a communist
5 all morality lies in this united discipline and conscious mass struggle against the exploiters. We do not believe in an eternal morality.

The belief of Lenin and the Bolsheviks that they were the special agents of historical change led logically to their destruction of all other political parties. Since history was on their side, the Bolsheviks had the right to absolute control. Initially, there were protests from within the Bolshevik Party over this. Some members, who had hoped that Bolshevik rule would be both socialist and democratic, were disturbed by Lenin's assumption that he was entitled to direct the lives of the ordinary people of Russia. Maxim Gorky warned:

1 Lenin is a gifted man who has all the qualities of a leader, including these essential ones: lack of morality and a merciless, lordly harshness towards the lives of the masses. As long as I can, I will repeat to the Russian proletariat, 'You are being led to destruction, you are being
5 used as material in an inhuman experiment; to your leaders, you are not human.'

3 Lenin's Legacy

KEY ISSUE What legacy did Lenin leave the USSR?

Gorky's warning raises the question which historians once hotly debated: whether the brutal totalitarianism of the Stalinist regime which operated from the late 1920s was the responsibility solely of

Stalin, or whether it was a logical development of the system previously established under Lenin. What can now be said is that the
6,724 letters in Lenin's private correspondence which became available for scrutiny in the 1990s reveal that the brutal methods which
Lenin adopted after 1917 caused him no qualms. In reviewing Robert
Service's biography, Dominic Lieven concludes that Lenin was motiv-
ated by hatred. He writes of:

1 Lenin's huge visceral hatred for old Russia: for the Romanov's of course
   above all and for the old upper and middle classes, but also for the
   whole of old Russian culture ... In no circumstances would 20th-cen-
   tury Russian history have been pleasant or bloodless. But Lenin made it
5 far worse than it needed to be. In 1917 he combined fanaticism, ruthlessness and absolute self-confidence with a terrifying naivety about
   government, economics and Russian society. His gamble on international revolution failed but even had it succeeded it would probably
   in time have established bitterly hostile, rival Marxist factions in power
10 in Berlin and Moscow. To impose such immense sacrifices in the name
   of so naive and flawed a vision makes Lenin one of the greatest criminals of the 20th century.[1]

Scholars now emphasise that the principal instruments of Stalin's
tyranny were already in existence by the time of Lenin's death. The
one-party state, the secret police, the ban on factionalism (which
effectively prohibited criticism of government or party policy), the
destruction of the trade unions as an independent force representing
the workers: these totalitarian features had all come into being by
1924.
    It is also true that under Lenin's guidance the first steps had been
taken towards institutionalising the 'purge', the system of ruthless
suppression of opposition by means of public show trials. Purges were
to be the outstanding feature of Stalin's terror strategy, but their
mechanism was already in place by 1924. The first show trial was conducted in the USSR in 1922, when, under the measures creating the
one-party state introduced by Lenin in 1921 at the Tenth Party
Congress, a group of SRs were publicly tried and condemned. At the
time of the trial, Lenin wrote to the commissar for justice: 'In my
opinion it is necessary to extend the death penalty by shooting to all
types of conspiratorial activity.'
    For the last two years of his life Lenin's physical frailty seriously
limited his control over events. There were signs that he was angered
or dismayed by many of the developments within the government and
the party but was too unwell to prevent them. His views on the leading Bolsheviks were neither complimentary nor optimistic. In a series
of dictated notes, known as his 'Last Will and Testament', he was
sharply critical of his colleagues: Trotsky, Stalin and Bukharin were
singled out as having serious character faults or political weaknesses.
However, Lenin made no provision for what should follow after his

death. He intimated that some form of collective leadership might be adopted, but he gave no clear instructions as to how this was to be organised. This made a power struggle after his death unavoidable.

As an international revolutionary, Lenin had originally expected that the successful Bolshevik seizure of power in October 1917 would be the first stage in a worldwide proletarian uprising. When this proved mistaken, he had to adjust to a situation in which Bolshevik Russia became an isolated revolutionary state, beset by internal and external enemies. This involved him in another major reformulation of Marxist theory. Marx had taught that proletarian revolution would be an international class movement. Yet the 1917 Revolution had been the work not of a class but of a party and had been restricted to one nation. Lenin explained this in terms of a delayed revolution; the international rising would occur at some point in the future; in the interim Soviet Russia must consolidate its own individual revolution. This placed the Bolshevik government and its international agency, the Comintern, in an ambiguous position. What was their essential role to be? At Lenin's death, this question – whether the USSR's primary aim was world revolution or national survival – was still unresolved.

4 Interpretations of the Russian Revolution

> **KEY ISSUES** On what main points did the major interpretations of the Russian Revolution differ between 1917 and 1991? How have attitudes towards the Russian Revolution changed since the collapse of the USSR in 1991?

The Russian Revolution was an extraordinary political, social and economic experiment. The collapse of Communism in Russia in the early 1990s seemed to indicate the experiment had failed. But that served only to increase interest in the subject. In the 1990s more books were published on the Russian Revolution than in any previous decade. The following paragraphs list the major interpretations between 1917 and the present. There have been so many important studies of the theme that the listing is necessarily a very selective one. Nevertheless, although it does not include all the theories that have been put forward, it does indicate some of the principal approaches. The list is divided into two main sections: 1) the major interpretations between 1917 and the collapse of the USSR in 1991, and 2) those that have developed since 1991.

1. a) **The traditional Soviet view** – based on the writings of Lenin, that the Russian Revolution was part of an inevitable scientific process and that it marked the seizure of power by the Russian masses, led by the Marxist-inspired Bolshevik Party, which then went on to create a workers' state. This was the only view permitted in the USSR until the 1990s. Soviet historians were state employees who were required to be active promoters of the Revolution not detached observers. A typical expression of their official approach was given in 1960 by the Academy of Sciences, the Soviet body which controlled historical publications: 'The study of history has never been a mere curiosity, a withdrawal into the past for the sake of the past. Historical science has been and remains an arena of sharp ideological struggle and remains a class, party history'.

b) The theory of 'the unfinished revolution' – associated particularly with the ideas of Trotsky – which argued that a genuine workers' revolution occurred in 1917, but was later betrayed by Lenin's successors. According to this school of thought, which was powerfully represented in the West by such writers as Isaac Deutscher and Adam Ulam, the initial revolutionary achievement of the workers was destroyed by the deadening rule of the bureaucratic and repressive Communist Party of the Soviet Union (CPSU) under Stalin.

c) The 'Optimist' view – favoured by Russian *émigrés* (those who fled abroad to escape the Revolution) and held by such historians as George Katkov, that imperial Russia was steadily transforming itself into a modern, democratic, industrial society until weakened by the 1914–17 war and subverted by the Bolsheviks, who were in the pay of the German government.

d) The 'Pessimist' view – In the 1960s, Leopold Haimson had a major impact on studies of the Revolution. He advanced the notion that, far from moving towards modernisation, imperial Russia had been heading towards revolutionary turmoil. He argued that the First World War made little difference. Russia was suffering an institutional crisis. So wide was the gap between the reactionary privileged tsarist establishment and the progressive professional classes and urban workers that Russia had become irrevocably polarised. Revolution was the unavoidable outcome.

e) The post-glasnost Soviet view – developed during the years of the Gorbachev reforms of the late 1980s. It approached Russian history in a more open-minded way and admitted that mistakes were made by the Bolsheviks. The leading exponent of this interpretation was Dmitri Volkogonov, whose analysis of Stalinism concluded that Stalin's tyranny was a product of the authoritarianism of Lenin and the Bolsheviks after 1917. Volkogonov paid tribute to the work of the western historians, Leonard Schapiro and Robert Conquest, both of whom had originally been sympathetic to Soviet Communism but whose subsequent researches led them to depict it as essentially oppressive.

2. Post-Soviet revisionism – The collapse of the Communist Party and the disintegration of the USSR in the 1990s had a profound impact on historical thinking. Interpretation is rarely neutral. The way historians view the past is affected by their experiences of the present. The survival of Soviet Russia for nearly 75 years had helped to give strength to the Marxist analysis of history. The very existence of this Communist state was claimed by its supporters to be proof that it had come into being in conformity with the dilectical laws of the class war. But once the USSR had broken up it became much harder to justify this determinist view of history. After 1991 those writers on Russia who had never accepted the concept of history being governed by laws regained their confidence. Without denying the obvious importance of economic and social trends, they reasserted the importance of what individuals and groups had actually done. The Russian Revolution had unfolded the way it had, not in accordance with social or economic laws, but because individuals and groups had chosen to behave in a particular way rather than in another.

Such views were given added academic respectability by the second major result of the fall of Communism in 1991 – the opening of the Russian archives. The new non-Communist government allowed access to the hundreds of thousands of documents that had lain unexamined in the Soviet state archives during the previous 75 years. Before he died in 1995, Volkoganov used these to write an iconoclastic trilogy of biographies on Lenin, Stalin and Trotsky. A number of Western scholars were also permitted to study the Russian documentary treasure trove. Robert Service's own biography of Lenin drew on the previously unseen Lenin manuscripts.

No single identifiable viewpoint has yet emerged. Indeed, outstanding modern historians, such as Orlando Figes, Richard Pipes and Robert Service differ on a whole range of issues. But where they share common ground is in taking a non-determinist approach. In Russia nothing was pre-ordained, nothing absolutely had to happen the way it did. Politics was crucial. Things occurred the way they did because of the decisions made by the participants. The following two extracts illustrate this viewpoint: the first is from Richard Pipes, the second from Orlando Figes:

> The Russian Revolution was made neither by the forces of nature nor by anonymous masses but by identifiable men pursuing their own advantage. Although it had spontaneous aspects, in the main it was the result of deliberate action.[2]

> I have tried to present the revolution not as a march of social forces and ideologies, but as a human event of complicated individual tragedies. It was a story by and large of people like the figures in this book setting out with high ideals only to achieve one thing only to find out later that
> 5   the outcome was quite different.[3]

History, of course, as these writers are the first to acknowledge, is a two-way process. Nobody can start from scratch; they have to work within the existing circumstances. It was Marx himself who had said that 'men make their own history but not in conditions of their own choosing'.

This survey of the interpretations of the Russian Revolution should give you some idea that there is nothing fixed about our understanding of 1917 and the developments that preceded and followed it. You may care to use the survey of the main schools of thought as a set of reference points for checking against the various historical disputes that have been introduced in this book.

Summary Diagram
Russia in 1881 and in 1924

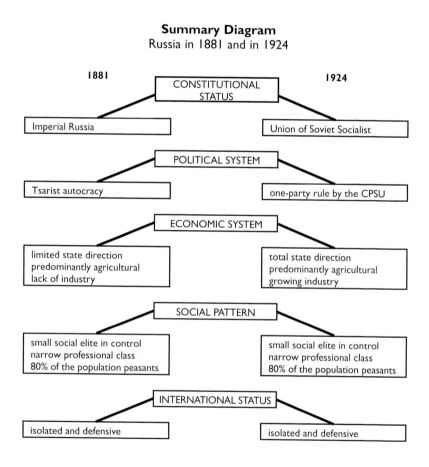

References:

1   Dominic Lieven in *The Sunday Telegraph,* 12 March 2000
2   Richard Pipes, *The Russian Revolution 1899–1919* (Collins Harvill, 1990) p.xxiv
3   Orlando Figes, *A People's Tragedy The Russian Revolution 1891–1924* (Johnathan Cape, 1996) p.xvii

Working on Chapter 8

The conclusion offers three main arguments:

1. Despite the upheavals of war and revolution there is a strong continuity in the Russian history of this period.
2. The Bolshevik *coup* in October 1917 did not mark a real break with the past, since, although the form of government changed, its essentially authoritarian and non-representative character did not.
3. 1917 was not a victory for Marxism, since Lenin in his leadership and consolidation of the Revolution did not follow or fulfil strict Marxist theory.

It would help you to ensure that you have acquired an effective overview of the topic if you were to test the validity of these three propositions by measuring them against your understanding of the earlier chapters of the book, and by asking yourself how far they accord with the viewpoints of the other writers whose work you have studied on this period.

The points of continuity and change in Russian history in this period are represented in chart form comparing the situation in 1881 with that in 1924. It is worth asking yourself which are the more impressive or important – the similarities or the differences?

Further Reading

The following is a selective list from the huge number of studies on Russia in the period covered by this book. Where possible, reference is to the latest paperback edition.

1. General Surveys

Two authoritative surveys are **Geoffrey Hosking's**, *A History of the Soviet Union, Final edition* (Fontana, 1992) and **Robert Service**, *A History of Twentieth-Century Russia* (Allen Lane, 1998). A sound text which introduces the key issues is **Michael Kort's**, *The Soviet Colossus: History and Aftermath* (M.E.Sharpe, 1996). Older books of value as introductions are **J.N. Westwood's**, *Endurance and Endeavour: Russian History, 1812–1980* (OUP, 1973) and **L. Kochan's**, *The Making of Modern Russia* (Penguin, 1977). Arguably, the leading contemporary authority on modern Russian history is the Polish-American scholar **Richard Pipes**. His major works, which between them cover the period, are: *Russia Under the Old Regime* (Penguin, 1987), *The Russian Revolution 1899–1919* (Collins Harvill, 1990), and *Russia Under the Bolshevik Regime* (Collins Harvill, 1994). These should be compared with an outstanding analysis by a British historian, **Orlando Figes**, *A People's Tragedy: The Russian Revolution 1891–1924* (Jonathan Cape, 1996). This book is a must for all students. It has made a major impact on the study of the revolution and has been widely hailed as a comprehensive and authoritative account of the events and issues arising from the period. Its kaleidoscopic approach offers endless insights into revolutionary Russia. One of Figes' strengths is that he had access to the Russian archives that were opened to scholars in the 1990s following the collapse of the USSR. Students are encouraged to compare Figes' and Pipes' books with the leading study from an older generation: **E.H. Carr**, *The Bolshevik Revolution, 1917–23* (first published by Macmillan in 1950 as part of a multi-volume history of Soviet Russia). Despite its title, the work analyses the period from 1898 onwards. There is a also a convenient single volume: *The Russian Revolution from Lenin to Stalin, 1917–29* (Macmillan, 1979), whose earlier chapters cover the pre-1917 period. **Sheila Fitzpatrick's**, *The Russian Revolution, 1917–32* (OUP, 1982) has become a standard text, as has **Beryl Williams'**, *The Russian Revolution, 1917–32* (Blackwell, 1987). A very helpful collection of potted biographies is to be found in **Martin McCauley's** *Who's Who in Russian History since 1900* (Routledge, 1997). An outstanding source study of the period, which includes a number of previously unseen Russian documents, is **Richard Sakwa's** *The Rise and Fall of the Soviet Union, 1917–1991* (Routledge, 1999). Perhaps the most absorbing survey is by the ex-Soviet Communist historian, **Dmitri Volkogonov,** who in the 1990s produced a trilogy of biographies on Lenin, Trotsky and Stalin, and who just before his death in 1995 completed, *The Rise and Fall of the*

Soviet Empire: Political Leaders from Lenin to Gorbachev (Harper Collins, 1997).

2. Particular Themes

Students need to appreciate the great importance of economics in the development of Russia in this period. The most accessible study, which begins with an analysis of the economy of imperial Russia, remains: **Alec Nove**, *An Economic History of the USSR* (Penguin, 1976). Other important studies are **W.E. Mosse**, *An Economic History of Russia 1856–1914* (Tauris, 1996), **P.R. Gregory**, *Before Command* (Princeton, 1994), **R.W. Davies**, *From Tsarism to the New Economic Policy* (Cornell UP, 1991), and **Peter Gatrell**, *The Tsarist Economy* (Batsford, 1986). One of the most readable accounts of the collapse of the Romanovs is still: **Hugh Seton Watson**, *The Decline of Imperial Russia* (Methuen, 1952). This should be supplemented with **R.B. McKean's**, *The Russian Constitutional Monarchy 1907–1917* (Blackwell, 1977) and **Dominic Lieven's**, *Russia's Rulers Under the Old Regime* (New York, 1989). The last author's *Russia and the Origins of the First World War* (Macmillan, 1983) deals illuminatingly with late tsarist foreign policy. Students wishing to understand the details of imperial Russia's war effort are likely to be stimulated by the treatment of the theme by an outstanding, if controversial, modern historian: **Norman Stone**, *The Eastern Front* (Hodder and Stoughton, 1975). **Richard Pipes'** latest reflections on 1917 are in his *Three Whys of the Russian Revolution* (Pimlico, 1998). **Martin McCauley's**, *The Russian Revolution and the Soviet State 1917–1921* (Macmillan, 1980) deals with the Bolshevik consolidation of power after the October coup. The struggle of the Bolsheviks to survive after 1917 is also the theme of **E. Mawdsley's**, *The Russian Civil War* (Allen and Unwin, 1987), a book which is much more than a military history. Fascinating treatments of the tsarist and the Bolshevik secret police are **Charles A. Rudd & Sergei A. Sepnaov**, *Fontanka 16: the Tsars' Secret Police* (Sutton, 1999) and **George Leggett**, *The Cheka: Lenin's Political Police* (OUP, 1981). Although written before the Russian archives were opened, **Edward Acton's** *Rethinking the Russian Revolution* (Arnold, 1990) is a highly informative analysis of the changing interpretations of the Russian Revolution. Cultural aspects of the Revolution are addressed in **Orlando Figes & Boris Kolonitskii**, *Interpreting the Russian Revolution: The Language and Symbols of 1917* (Yale, 1999) and **Sheila Fitzpatrick**, *The Cultural Front Power and Culture in Revolutionary Russia* (Cornell, 1992). An important set of essays introducing many of the latest research findings on politics and society in this period is in **Ian D. Thatcher** (ed), *Regime and Society in Twentieth-Century Russia* (Macmillan, 1999)

3. Biographies

The most readable biography of the last of the Romanovs is **Dominic Lieven**, *Nicholas II: Emperor of All the Russias* (London, 1993). Also interesting are **R.K. Massie's**, *The Romanovs: The Final Chapter* (London, 1995) and **E. Radzinsky**, *The Last Tsar: The Life and Death of Nicholas II* (London, 1992). The most informed and best balanced book on 'the mad monk' is **Brian Moynahan's**, *Rasputin: the Saint Who Sinned* (Aurum, 1998). An important book on an important figure is **Richard Abraham's**, *Alexander Kerensky: The First Love of the Revolution* (New York, 1987). Lenin of course remains the dominant figure of the period. A helpful brief introduction is **John Laver's** *Lenin* (Hodder & Stoughton, 1993). Worth singling out from the many important studies of him are **Tony Cliff**, *Lenin* (Bookmarks, 1987), which is sympathetic towards its subject, and **David Shub's**, *Lenin* (Penguin, 1966), which is a hostile treatment by one of Lenin's SD contemporaries. However, interesting as those books are, they have been superseded by **Dmitri Volkogonov's**, *Lenin Life and Legacy* (Harper Collins, 1994) and **Robert Service's**, *Lenin A Biography* (Macmillan, 2000), both studies being based fully on the new archival material. Valuable for the same reason is **Richard Pipes**, (ed), *The Unknown Lenin: From the Soviet Archives* (Yale, 1996). Despite having been treated in Stalin's Russia as a 'non-person', Trotsky has been reinstated as the organiser of the October Revolution. A useful short introduction is **Michael Lynch's** *Trotsky the Permanent Revolutionary* (Hodder & Stoughton, 1995). A very long, but very valuable biography is **Isaac Deutscher**, *Trotsky* (OUP, 3 volumes, 1954–70). **Dmitri Volkogonov's**, *Stalin Triumph and Tragedy* (Weidenfeld and Nicholson, 1991) and *Trotsky the Eternal Revolutionary* (Free Press, 1996) completed his great trilogy of the makers of the Russian Revolution.

Glossary

Bolshevik	The name (meaning 'majority') taken by Lenin and his followers after the split in the SD Party in 1903.
Bourgeoisie	The Marxist term for the exploiting capitalist middle class.
Bund	An organisation formed by revolutionary Jews in tsarist Russia.
CCCP	Central Committee of the Communist Party.
Cheka	All Russian Extraordinary Commission for Fighting Counter-Revolution (the Bolshevik secret police).
Comintern	The Communist International organisation, established in 1919 for the purpose of bringing about revolution in other countries.
Commissar	Minister or official in the Soviet government or CPSU.
CPSU	The Communist Party of the Soviet Union (formerly the Bolshevik Party).
Diktat	A settlement imposed by threat of force.
Duma	The imperial Russian parliament between 1906 and 1917.
Emigrés	Those who fled Russia to avoid government oppression.
Ghetto	The Jewish quarters in a town or city.
Glasnost	Russian for 'openness', adopted as a description of the new Soviet approach of the late 1980s and 1990s.
GOELRO	A special state commission, established in 1920 to organise the electrification of Russia.
Gosplan	Superseded *Vesenkha* in 1921 as the body responsible for integrated national economic planning.
Intelligentsia	The educated and more enlightened members of Russian society, who were usually supporters of reform.
Iskra	Russian for 'the spark', an SD newspaper, founded by Lenin and Martov in 1898.
Izvestiya	Russian for 'the news', taken as the title of a main Bolshevik newspaper.
Kadets (KDs)	The Constitutional Democrats, a liberal party, founded in 1905.
Kolkhozy	The collective farms.
Konsomol	The Young Communist League, a movement for young people between the ages of 14 and 28.
Kulaks	The class of rich peasants.
Marxism/ Leninism	The official Bolshevik/Communist ideology based on the theories of Karl Marx.

Mensheviks	The word (meaning minority) used to describe the followers of Plekhanov after the split in the SD Party in 1903.
Mir	The village commune.
MRC	The military revolutionary committee of the Petrograd soviet.
Narkomprod	The People's Commission of Supply.
Narodniks	Russian for 'the people', the Populist movement that looked to the peasants to take the lead in the transforming of Russia.
NEP	The New Economic Policy, introduced by Lenin in 1921.
Nepmen	The class of merchants and middlemen who profited from the NEP.
Octobrists	The moderate reformist party, established in 1905.
Okhrana (Okhranka)	The tsarist secret police.
Orgburo	The CCCP's bureau of organisation.
Pogroms	Organised persecutions of the Jews.
Politburo	The Political Bureau, the inner cabinet of the CCCP.
Pravda	Russian for truth, taken as the title of a Bolshevik newspaper, established in 1912.
Proletariat	The Marxist term for the revolutionary working class.
RSFSR	The Russian Socialist Federal Soviet Republic, the title of the Soviet state between 1918 and 1922.
Stavka	The high command of the imperial Russian army.
SDs	The Social-Democratic Workers' Party which divided into Bolshevik and Menshevik wings in 1903.
Sovkhozy	The state collective farms.
Sovnarkom	The Council of People's Commissars (the government of the USSR).
SRs	The Social Revolutionary Party, which developed out of the Populist movement.
Trudoviks	The labour group on the moderate wing of the SRs.
USSR	The Union of Soviet Socialist Republics, which became the official title of the Soviet state after 1922.
Verst	A unit of measurement (two-thirds of a mile).
Vesenkha	The Supreme Council of the National Economy.
Vyperod	Russian for 'forward', adopted by Lenin as the title of a Bolshevik journal.
Zemgor	The union of municipal councils and *zemstva* that combined in 1914 to further the Russian war effort.
Zemstva	Local government councils in the countryside, established in 1864.

Index